C000129899

"As always, Alan's books are such ~~explanation and pastoral encouragem~~ the heart and the mind in a beauti Knowing and working with him these pages is what you'll hear him speaking about with passion across the kitchen table from you! Truly wonderful stuff!"

Johnny Markin

Johnny is Emeritus Pastor of Worship Ministries at Northview Community Church, Abbottsford BC, overseeing the development of worship leaders and team training, and leading worship at various venues. He is also seconded to Trinity Western University, where he is an adjunct Instructor in the Worship Arts Department, developing leaders and instructing in worship theology.

"Alan is a Bible teacher. He doesn't just read the Bible, he studies and researches each passage he reads. Why does he do this? For two main reasons, I think. Firstly, because he wants to get to know God and his Word better himself, and secondly, so that he can share what he has learnt with others so they too can enjoy a similar experience. I recommend that you invest in this book; it really will bring Paul's letter to the Philippians alive in a new and refreshing way."

Ishmael

Ishmael is well known for his children's ministry over several decades and has written and recorded over 400 songs (including 'Father God I Wonder') and released around 40 albums of his own and other writers' songs, having produced 15 of these. He has also released 5 music DVDs. Ishmael was ordained into the Anglican Church in 2007 and is now licensed to Chichester Cathedral as their non-stipendiary 'Missioner Deacon' and is affectionately known to the Bishop, Dean and Chapter, and congregation as 'Deacon Ish!'

"Alan gives us distilled nuggets of wisdom in his latest commentary. As always, Jesus is at the centre of Alan's thoughts and you will benefit from his deep personal relationship with the Saviour. I highly recommend his book!"

Laurie Mellor

Laurie is the founder of, and jointly heads, the Mellor Practice, with almost 40 years' experience in financial services. He has particular strengths in the area of investment, having invested over £85 million for clients over the years. He combines caution with a flair for emerging markets. He is the author of three published books, one of them being 'The Sick Rose' – a refreshing and challenging look at the spiritual history and life of the church in Great Britain.

"One of the most valuable gifts we can ever be given is sound, loving spiritual guidance. With keen insight, Alan leads his readers into, through and beyond Paul's most encouraging of letters, so that we can taste the joy for ourselves. We are the richer for this care-full, Spirit-breathed study, and will want to pray more diligently and reach out more boldly in the light of it."

Rev. Ian Silk

Ian Silk is a Pastor, Teacher, Missioner and Researcher. He holds degrees in Classics and Theology and has ministered in Cambridge, Lincoln and East Africa. Ian's doctoral studies explore the dynamics of mission team life in the New Testament, church history and contemporary practice.

"Alan Hoare is my 'go to' friend in ministry. He is a 'pastor's pastor'! He exudes wisdom honed through the years of faithfully serving and listening to God. He is a rare breed. Alan is a Spirit-filled, fully-signed-up Evangelical mystic. He, like the mystics of old, has learnt to 'settle himself in silence' and become absorbed in simply 'being'. His joy in the written Word of God is infectious. Enjoy the writings of this scholarly, kind and gentle man."

Rev. Canon Chris Bowater OSL

Chris is considered by many to be a father of the modern worship movement. Coming to prominence in the Charismatic renewal of the late 1970s and early 1980s, his songs have been translated into many languages and used in churches all over the world.

"Alan's rich exposition of Scripture is both strengthening and challenging. As an author and teacher, his daily approach to unpacking Philippians reveals the wealth and depth of the Apostle Paul's letter, encouraging and teaching the followers of Jesus in genuine Christianity. Alan brings depth of meaning and practical application in language accessible for every believer in their pursuit of Christlike discipleship."

Mark Watson

Mark Watson is senior pastor of Sleaford New Life Church, a Ground Level church in southern Lincolnshire. Originally from Norwich, Mark and his wife Susan have served in leadership in local church for many years with an emphasis in the worship arena. Mark is a graduate of CFNi Dallas, and is passionate about growing disciples through God's Word.

"It is a delight and a privilege to be able to recommend Alan's latest book to you. He writes from the heart of a man who has an intense love and passion not just for the Word of God but for the Author of the Word, in whose company he has spent much time. I have never failed to be touched by the gracious way in which Alan opens the Word of God to the people of God. In this book you will, like the man in Jesus' parable, find great treasure that will enrich your soul and expand your spiritual horizons."

Dr Bob Duerden

Bob holds a PhD in seaweed ecology. He entered the teaching profession, becoming head of a large science department. After transferring to advisory work, he became senior advisor for East Yorkshire. Upon retirement he became a part time consultant for the Diocese of York's education team. Bob has served in both Anglican and New Churches, taking up leadership roles with a teaching responsibility. He still supports his local church in Sleaford. He is supported in ministry by his wife, Penel.

"Alan finds a way to reach busy God-seeking Christians in his books that makes the key messages accessible and applicable immediately. He balances his knowledge carefully to let us know just enough detail to ground-truth the setting of the story, and on which he builds his message, providing insight into the world view at the time of writing. He then uses his quiet and deeply won wisdom to connect the message to challenges we face, and what we can learn from this and apply to our lives today. He seems to just catch the right balance of head (information and analysis), with heart (longings), with gut (knowing what to do), in a way that guides us to pursue our path to God."

Dr John-Henry Lonie

John-Henry hold a PhD in Science. He specialises in physiological, chemical and statistical plant ecology. He founded and heads up Sustainable Direction Ltd, providing business solutions that help private companies, non-profit organisations and public agencies improve environmental and sustainability performance. He draws on decades of distinctive, high-quality environmental and sustainability experience and expertise to respond with agility to client needs. He is also an active elder in his local church.

Onwards and Upwards Publishers

3 Radfords Turf, Cranbrook, Exeter, EX5 7DX.

www.onwardsandupwards.org

First edition (2019) published in the UK by Onwards and Upwards Publishers Ltd.

ISBN: 978-1-78815-693-6

Typeface: Sabon LT

Graphic design: LM Graphic Design / Ben Hoare

PHILIPPIANS

My Favourite Church

A daily study of the letter of Paul to the church at Philippi

Alan Hoare

O&U
Onwards & Upwards

About the Author

Alan was born in Rustington in West Sussex in 1948, and soon after the family moved to Littlehampton. This was followed by two younger brothers, Nigel and Simon. His first experience of church at the age of ten years old ended a few weeks later by him being banned from the local Sunday school for bad behaviour! Also during his final years at secondary school, he boycotted the RE lessons for two years, feeling that they were getting too personal! After leaving school he did an apprenticeship in precision engineering, gaining City and Guilds certificates at Worthing Technical College. It was the 'hippy' era of the 1960s, so weekends were spent with friends, often performing in their rock band, aptly named the 'St James' Infirmary'. A favourite pastime of his is still to pick up his guitar and play the music of that era.

Life changed dramatically for him in March 1969 when he became a Christian as the result of visiting a small Free Church in the little village of Fittleworth, near Petworth. Soon after that, the Baptist Church in Littlehampton became his home church, and also the place where he met Maureen (affectionately known as Mo), who was to become his wife in 1974. Before that, however, they parted company for two years – he to work on a church planting team with Operation Mobilisation in France for two years, and she to do teacher training in Portsmouth.

On returning to England in 1973, Alan studied theology at the Elim Bible College, which was then in Dorking in Surrey, graduating two years later with a Diploma in Theology. Marriage took place in the middle of the course – which was highly unusual in those days! This was followed by two years in London, during which time he was an assistant minister at two Elim Pentecostal churches, helped to pioneer two more churches and had two children: Ruth, who was born prematurely in August 1975, and Joseph, who was born in February 1977.

August 1977 saw a move to Lincoln, where he took up the pastorate of an Elim Pentecostal church for nearly ten years. The family meanwhile continued to grow with the added births of Simon in November 1980 and Sarah in March 1982.

In Lincoln, Alan quickly developed a strong connection with Stuart Bell, the leader of the large and growing New Life Church there (now 'Alive Church'), and was one of the founder members of the Ground Level network of churches which Stuart started and still leads. In 1987 he joined the New Life Church himself, serving as a member until 1991, when he joined the staff as part of the leadership team. His role was to head up the pastoral and teaching ministry of the church. Benjamin, his youngest son, was born in November that year, completing their family – a biblical quiver full!

In his work for Alive church, Alan has also, amongst other things, pastored a number of linked congregations around the area, written and delivered staff devotions, and led marriage preparation, baptismal and membership courses. From 2003, he wrote and delivered biblical courses, firstly at the New Life church, and then in a number of different church settings. These 'X-Plore' classes ran for 16 years, and topics covered included, amongst others, 'The Life and Times of Christ', 'The Life and Times of David', 'The Life of the Apostle Paul', 'Spiritual Theology', 'Systematic Theology' and 'Church History'. He has also delivered expositional lectures on the letters of Paul to the Philippians and Ephesians. For a number of years, he was also a contributor for Scripture Union's online WordLive daily devotions.

Alan had always dreamt of studying for a degree in theology, and was delighted when the church released him for one day a week in 2009 so that he could do this. He attended Mattersey Hall near Doncaster, and was accepted on to the Master's course, graduating three years later with a Master's in practical theology.

In 2011, he reduced his time at Lincoln to three days a week, and took on a new role as the senior pastor of a thriving church in Kirton, near Boston, some forty miles east of Lincoln. After three years working for them two days a week, he helped them with the transition to a new senior pastor, and remained on their leadership team serving as their teaching pastor.

On reaching retirement age in August 2013, Alan retired completely from the staff at Lincoln, and was able to devote himself more to study, writing and teaching. In 2019, he retired from the New Life Community church in Kirton, but still remains on their Leadership team, visiting the church once a month on a Sunday to preach.

Over the years, he has ministered widely in the UK and also abroad in Mozambique, Vietnam, Cambodia, France, Spain, Poland and Greece.

Alan feels that his ministry is primarily about building strong and deep spiritual foundations. Strong and mature churches, in his view, are made up of strong and mature believers. He teaches about developing a close and mature walk with Christ, believing that spiritual roots are essential to growing a healthy Christian life. He is passionate about getting people to read the Bible for themselves!

Alan and Mo have now been married for forty-five years, and have seen their five children grow up into fine adults. They have, to date, eleven grandchildren!

Alan Hoare can be contacted by email:

alanerichoare@gmail.com

To see all the author's books published by Onwards and Upwards, visit his author page:

www.onwardsandupwards.org/alan-hoare

Or scan the barcode below with your phone:

Acknowledgements

I would like to thank, first of all, my wife Mo, for her many years of loyal love, encouragement and support. She has been, and still is, a pillar of strength to me.

I would like to thank Laurie Mellor, Director at The Mellor Practice Ltd, who has faithfully trawled through the manuscript, correcting and making several essential and helpful recommendations.

I would also like to thank my publisher, Luke Jeffery, of Onwards and Upwards Publishers, for both his constant encouragement and hard work in making my book-writing dreams happen.

Purpose of this Book

There are three main purposes for the format of this book, as well as the other two that I have written.[1]

The first reason is that I wanted to provide a daily devotional that would work through a whole book of the Bible (or a whole Psalm as in the first book). This devotional commentary both exegetes and explains the text, and then seeks to apply it to everyday living.

The second reason is that once finished, the reader is left with a complete commentary on the book, which can be referred to at other times.

The third reason is to introduce the reader to a systematic reading of the Scripture for themselves. Hopefully, going through this book will whet the appetite to start digging out the incredible riches and treasures that are found, not only on the surface, but just underneath.

---

[1] Alan Hoare, *The Song in the Gate,* (Onwards and Upwards, Leatherhead, 2015); Alan Hoare, *Shoe Leather Faith,* (Onward and Upwards, Exeter, 2017)

What Others Have Said About This Letter

Written as it was under the shadow of a dark and ominous cloud, the epistle resounds with the note of joy. It is one of the priceless treasures of the Christian Church. To countless pilgrims on the way of life it has brought comfort and strength, and it will continue to so to do so long as life shall last.

Dr Rev. J. Hugh Michael D.D.[1]

Philippians is a joyful letter, but its undercurrent is a sober realization that time is running out.

J.A. Motyer[2]

A very intimate relationship seems to have existed between the apostle and the Church, where the first fruits of Europe were gathered by him for Christendom... [this is the] most personal of all letters of Paul.

Dr Jac J. Müller[3]

This is Paul's happiest letter.

Eugene Peterson[4]

Except possibly for the letter to Philemon, this is the most personal example of Paul's correspondence, and he is obviously fond of the little church at Philippi.

J.B. Phillips[5]

---

[1] J. Hugh Michael, *The Epistle of Paul to the Philippians,* (Hodder & Stoughton, London, 1934), p.xxii
[2] Alec Motyer, *The Message of Philippians,* BST series, (IVP, Leicester, 1984), p.11
[3] Jac Müller, *The Epistles of Paul to the Philippians and to Philemon,* (Eerdmans, Michigan, 1980), pp.13,31
[4] Eugene Peterson, *The Message Bible,* (NavPress, Colorado, 2002), p.2135
[5] J.B. Phillips, *The New Testament in Modern English,* (Godfrey Bles, London, 1960), p.410

The church at Philippi had great significance for Paul, since it was the first church he founded in Europe.

Sean M. McDonough[1]

Of all the letters Paul wrote to the churches, this one stands out as being the most personal.

Homer A. Kent, Jr[2]

[1] Sean M. McDonough, *Introduction to Philippians – ESV Study Bible,* (Crossway Bibles, Illinois, 2008), p.2275
[2] Homer A. Kent, Jr, *Introduction to Philippians,* NIV Bible Commentary, Vol 2, (Hodder & Stoughton, London, 1994), p.789

Foreword by Stuart Bell

Having worked alongside Alan for many years, certain things immediately come to mind. Firstly, his gentle deep desire to authentically follow Jesus, secondly his passionate love for the Bible and thirdly his eager desire to pass onto others what he has learnt through his pastoral ministry in the life of the church.

In this daily devotional these three things are very apparent. I encourage you to dedicate a hundred days to travel through Paul's letter to the Philippians. Each day carefully builds a picture of the content of the letter and gives opportunity to reflect and personally apply the teaching. Each day is unrushed, often applying one or two simple lessons.

However, over the hundred days of study, I believe two things will have happened; a daily disciplined love for serious study will have been established and the content and heart of one of Paul's most important letters unlocked in a life-changing way.

Thank you, Alan, for pursuing your life-long desire to help people see the value of developing daily devotions.

Stuart Bell BEM

Stuart Bell is the Senior Pastor of Alive Church, a growing multi-site church with several locations in the UK. He also leads the Ground Level Network, a network of around 90 churches and heads up 'Partners for Influence UK', a group of leaders representing influential churches and ministries across the UK. Stuart is actively involved in a number of national leadership forums and is an international speaker and teacher often working into both America and South Africa. Stuart has written four books.

DAY ONE

What's in a Name?

Acts 16:1,12

Paul came also to Derbe and to Lystra. A disciple was there, named Timothy, the son of a Jewish woman who was a believer, but his father was a Greek. ... So, setting sail from Troas, we made a direct voyage to Samothrace, and the following day to Neapolis, and from there to Philippi, which is a leading city of the district of Macedonia and a Roman colony. We remained in this city some days.

Around AD 60/61, the church in Philippi, founded by the apostle Paul some eleven years previously, sent a messenger called Epaphroditus with some money for Paul, who was now imprisoned in Rome. It seems that while he was there, Epaphroditus fell dangerously ill, and news of it came back to the church. After he had eventually recovered, Paul decided to send him back with a letter.

Professor Beet wrote:

The joy caused by his return, and the effect of this wonderful letter when first read in the church of Philippi, are hidden from us. And we may almost say that with this letter the church itself passes from our view. To-day, in silent meadows, quiet cattle browse among the ruins which mark the site of what was once the flourishing Roman colony of Philippi, the home of the most attractive church of the apostolic age. But the name and fame and spiritual influence of that church will never pass. To myriads of men and women in every age and nation, the letter written in a dungeon at Rome, and carried along the Egnatian Way by an obscure Christian messenger, has been a divine light and a cheerful guide along the most rugged paths of life.[1]

---

[1]   Professor Beet, cited in *Easton's Bible Dictionary*, e-sword.net

We find the beginnings of this first European church[1] in Acts 16:11-40. In verse 12 Luke records that it was "a leading city of the district of Macedonia and a Roman colony". Behind those few words is a powerful history. The old Thracian city was first known as 'Crenides' – a word meaning 'the fountain'. Apparently, there were springs there that fed the local river. This is so significant. From earliest times, the city had naturally been a source of blessing to the surrounding areas. First there is the natural, and then comes the spiritual. (1.Cor.15:46) History was to be repeated.

In 360BC the city was taken by Philip of Chalcedon, father of the infamous Alexander the Great. Philip fortified the city and renamed it after himself. In 42BC, a famous battle was fought there. Two Roman generals, Antony and Octavian, defeated the troops of Brutus and Cassius – two of the assassins of Julius Caesar. Octavian then went on to become Caesar Augustus, under whose reign Jesus was born. It was this same Augustus who turned the city of Philippi into a Roman colony, where veteran Roman soldiers could settle.

After the defeat of Antony and Cleopatra in 31BC, the city was awarded the honour of being a self-governing and tax-free haven. By the time that Paul arrived, the city was a well-established "miniature Rome"[2]. There were very few Jews to be found there. In fact, the Jewish population was so small that there wasn't even a synagogue. No Jewish names at all are found in any of the lists of converts from Philippi. Among the Romans and the local people, however, Paul found some real veteran soldier spirits. They were hard, disciplined and fiercely loyal. This was a hard ground to break into, but once touched by the power of the kingdom of heaven, they became shining examples of loyalty and devotion to the region and beyond. These people were to become Paul's favourite church. They certainly became a source of refreshment to him.

Thought

Loyalty is not so much a spoken word, but is something that is long-term and demonstrated in attitude and action. (Prov.20:6, NASB)

---

[1]   Alec Motyer, *The Message of Philippians,* BST series, (IVP, Leicester, 1984), p.15
[2]   William Hendriksen, *The Epistle to the Philippians,* (Banner of Truth, Edinburgh, 1963), p.7

Prayer

Help me today to demonstrate a long-term loyalty in all my significant relationships.

DAY TWO

A Roundabout Way

Acts 15:36-41; 16:6-12

And after some days Paul said to Barnabas, "Let us return and visit the brothers in every city where we proclaimed the word of the Lord, and see how they are." Now Barnabas wanted to take with them John called Mark. But Paul thought best not to take with them one who had withdrawn from them in Pamphylia and had not gone with them to the work. And there arose a sharp disagreement, so that they separated from each other. Barnabas took Mark with him and sailed away to Cyprus, but Paul chose Silas and departed, having been commended by the brothers to the grace of the Lord. And he went through Syria and Cilicia, strengthening the churches. ... And they went through the region of Phrygia and Galatia, having been forbidden by the Holy Spirit to speak the word in Asia. And when they had come up to Mysia, they attempted to go into Bithynia, but the Spirit of Jesus did not allow them. So, passing by Mysia, they went down to Troas. And a vision appeared to Paul in the night: a man of Macedonia was standing there, urging him and saying, "Come over to Macedonia and help us." And when Paul had seen the vision, immediately we sought to go on into Macedonia, concluding that God had called us to preach the gospel to them. So, setting sail from Troas, we made a direct voyage to Samothrace, and the following day to Neapolis, and from there to Philippi, which is a leading city of the district of Macedonia and a Roman colony. We remained in this city some days.

When we look at what actually brought Paul to Philippi, we can see that preceding the mission into Macedonia was a series of division, confusion and obstruction. It is worth noting that not everything in the kingdom runs smoothly. Sometimes, things look like the back of a piece of tapestry – making no sense from our point of view, but making absolute sense from the divine point of view.

First there was the sharp division between Paul and Barnabas over John Mark. All three were affected by it. There were hurt and angry feelings, and a real sense of being robbed. One doesn't get over broken friendships that quickly. Paul would have carried that with him as he journeyed on.

Secondly, there was the confusion over direction. As they sought to proceed with the mission, it seems that God was blocking them. This happened twice. Looking carefully, we acknowledge the general command to go global with the mission. Jesus had said, "Go therefore and make disciples of all nations..." (Matt.28:19) He had also said, "Go into all the world and preach the gospel..." (Mk.16:15) But then there was the divine strategy, and it is here that we see a strategic note being introduced to the mission. It was if God was saying, "Not here, not now." We need to thank God for 'closed doors' because they can actually reveal 'open doors'. And in the middle of the dark night there came a God-given vision and a sense of direction. Paul saw the man from Macedonia beckoning him, and the team responded.

In Acts 16:11, we read that they "made a direct voyage..." This literally reads, "They sailed before the wind." This is very interesting. It seems, at first, that they were pushing 'against the wind' of the Spirit, but now they were sailing 'before the wind'. In other words, the wind was now in their sails. It is a good thing to learn how to discern where God is moving and where he isn't.

God guides us not only by vision, but also by circumstances, commonplace things, dark things, difficult things and even disappointing things.[1] Frederick Faber sang, "Thrice blest is he to whom is given the instinct that can tell that God is on the field, when he is most invisible."[2] We need to learn to read God in the darkness as well as the blazing light.

Paul wrote this letter from a prison cell. His new circumstances brought about a necessary adaptation. Instead of speaking and debating, his *modus operandi* became that of intercession, prayerful thinking and writing. Here is a challenge: In our desperate search for release in our own ministry, is it possible to miss something special that God wants to do in us and through us? Did the prison walls limit the workings of God in Paul? I think not. We need to learn to find God when things change, seemingly for the worse, in our personal worlds. Here, for Paul at least,

---

[1]   G. Campbell Morgan, *The Acts of the Apostles,* (Pickering & Inglis, London, 1946), p.293

[2]   Frederick W. Faber, *Workman of God,* (http://finestofthewheat.org/workman-of-god/)

his ministry took a new turn into eternal perspectives. The churches he planted have gone. His letters, however, remain with us today.

Thought

A series of closed doors could be actually leading you to the open door.

Prayer

Dear Lord, give me a sensitivity of spirit to see you in the perplexities of life.

DAY THREE

Functions and Roles (1)

Phil.1:1

Paul and Timothy, servants of Christ Jesus,
To all the saints in Christ Jesus who are at Philippi, with the
overseers and deacons...

The year was around AD 61, and Paul was now imprisoned in Rome. He would stay there for about two years. He had been walking with the Lord for over thirty years. But the prison walls did not limit Paul's apostolic mind and heart. The strategy simply changed instead. It seems that the letters to the Ephesians, Colossians, Philemon – and toward the end of the two years, Philippians – were written at this time.

Letter-writing in the first century AD was quite different to what we have today. Ancient letters would usually start with the writer's name, and then the names of the recipients of the letter. This would be followed by a greeting and a blessing, and then the main body of the letter.

In this particular verse, we see four groupings of people and two locations. Today, we will look at two of the groups of people and the two locations. The first group are "servants" (ESV/NIV). Paul used this term to describe himself and Timothy. On other occasions, he used the term "apostle", but here, he used the word "servant". The word is *douloi*, and it literally meant 'slaves', or 'those who were not free'. The word expressed the condition of those who had a master, or those who were at the control of another. For Paul, it was a title of humility, and it was also the hallmark of a genuine ministry. Paul was a servant of Christ and also a servant of others, both in relationship and attitude.

The second group of people were the "saints". This was one of Paul's favourite words that he used to describe believers in Christ. The word is *hagoi*, and it meant 'the holy ones', those who were 'devoted' or 'consecrated' to God. The radical idea of the word described that which was separated from a common usage to a sacred usage, and it answered to the Hebrew word *qôdesh* which meant 'holy, sacred, set apart, consecrated'. In other words, the "saints" were the different ones, the separated ones and the sacred ones. They were different to the world, separated from the world, sacred or consecrated to God, for the express purpose of manifesting the life of God to the world. When we take on the name, we also take on the responsibility of the meaning of the name.

We now look at the locations. It is significant to observe how Paul has phrased this sentence. These "saints" were located first of all in Christ Jesus, and then they were located in the city of Philippi. "In Christ" is a very real and dynamic sphere, and in Paul's view, all believers are first located in him before they are located in any geographical setting. It is so important to grasp this. According to his letter to the Ephesian believers, we have been raised with Christ into the heavenly places. This is where we live in the realms of our spirit. Our life, our resources and our life paradigms should issue from being in Christ, and from heaven. Physically we live in a particular location, but spiritually we are coming from somewhere else, seeking to bring the dynamics and life of the kingdom of heaven into our locality.

Don't let the circumstances of your physical surroundings swamp you; rather be filled, influenced and inspired by heaven.

Thought

What we see around us affects us more than we think. Look at the story found in 2.Kgs.6:8-19, in particular vv.15-17.

Prayer

Dear Holy Spirit, open my eyes to see the realities of the invisible world of the kingdom of heaven around me.

DAY FOUR

Functions and Roles (2)

Phil.1:1

To all the saints in Christ Jesus who are at Philippi, with the overseers and deacons...

The Philippian believers were firstly "in Christ", and then they were "in Philippi". Their spiritual location took precedence over their geographical location. The man who knows where he is coming from is the most effective in ministry into the world. Jesus knew that he had come from God, and he also knew that he was returning to God. (Jn.13:3) All his resources were from heaven. Alec Motyer wrote:

> *In Christ we become new people with new feelings, a new mind or way of looking at things, new encouragement or incentives to live as Christians should. There is a new way of looking at life, seeing His hand, and His sovereign will in all things.[1]*

It is heavenly perspectives and resources, not earthly perspectives and resources, that should inspire and resource us. We are called to be 'in the world', but we are also charged not to be 'of it'.

Paul now mentions two 'offices' that were in the church: "overseers" and "deacons". These offices were not titles for status; rather they were descriptions of function. Paul described these offices and the moral and spiritual qualifications for them in more detail in 1.Tim.3:1-13 and Tit.1:5-9. Of the 16 standards set out for the office of an overseer, only one has to do with aptitude for ministry. The other 15 are to do with lifestyle and character issues. We see here the priority of God.

To understand more fully these two functions, we have to look at the words. The word "overseers" is *episkopoi*, and it describes 'those who diligently watch over, those who have oversight'. In other words, they watch over and facilitate the activities of others. They are the trainers and releasers of ministries; they provide guidance, nourishment and

---

[1] Alec Motyer, *The Message of Philippians,* BST series, (IVP, Leicester, 1984), p.27

protection to the flock of God. These are spiritual directors exercising spiritual oversight. In the New Testament, the term is synonymous with "elder". (Acts 20:17,28).

The word "deacons" is *diakonoi*, and the word means 'those who serve'. As far as I can see it, this function has to do with the practical aspects and oversight of the church, releasing the spiritual leadership to spiritual oversight. The qualifications, however, are not so much practical abilities, but are more to do with wisdom, faith and anointing.

Another word used in the New Testament to describe such leaders is "pillars". (Gal.2:9). Pillars are 'weight bearers' – they are the 'support structure' of any church. Such leadership, then, is far more about responsibility than role. Leaders are to carry the spiritual weight of the fellowship, and they carry the people upon their hearts into the presence of God.

Those of us who are leaders need to recognise our unspoken influence. We are observed. We are relied upon and leaned upon. We are reference points. May God help us to be reliable, strong and mature, carrying weight and moving people forward in their walk with God.

Thought

Genuine leadership has more to do with a sense of responsibility rather than a need for status.

Prayer

Lord, help me to carry the flock of God on my heart and shoulders rather than a sense of my own importance.

DAY FIVE

The Greeting

Phil. 1:2

Grace to you and peace from God our Father and the Lord Jesus Christ.

How greetings have changed over the years! Today it's either "Yo!" or "Hi!", or just a nod, or just a grunt. Words are important, and the words that we speak to each other can have great power. They can either deflate us or empower us. With these two words – "grace" and "peace" – Paul took both very common words of greeting and transformed them. He did not replace them, but turned them into words that became transforming words. Christ always loves to enrich the commonplace, taking what is very ordinary and giving it deeper depths and greater influence. This greeting would bear no resemblance at all to the half-hearted "have a nice day" from our local takeaway restaurant, but contained power-filled words that carried a divine potency.

These two words form part of the greeting that is found in all 13 of his letters. The first word, translated "grace", is the Greek word *charis*, and enriches the normal greeting *charein*. Grace is the free, spontaneous, unprovoked and unearnt gift of God. You and I are in the kingdom today as a pure gift from God. And whereas *charein* would have been shared between friends only, God spoke the word *charis* to us, who were by nature his enemies. Someone has written, "Grace is getting what we don't deserve; mercy is not getting what we do deserve." So, when we speak grace to each other, we remind each other of God's grace, and we empower and encourage each other.

The second word is "peace". The Greek word is *eirēnē*, and it is firmly rooted in the Hebrew word *shâlôm*. This Hebrew word is a deep word, meaning "a harmonious state of the soul and mind [that] encourages the development of the faculties and powers"[1]. So, if grace is the gift of God, then peace is the first fruits of that gift. Classical Greek describes peace

---

[1] W.E. Vine, *Complete expository Dictionary of the Old Testament*, e-sword.net

as something 'that binds together', and in Christ, God binds us to himself, and starts to bind us into a heart and mind unity with each other. This peace is profound: it gives us peace with God, it gives us peace with each other, it gives us peace with ourselves and it gives us peace in our circumstance. It is not the absence of conflict; but rather, it is the infusion of the tranquillity of heaven invading, guarding and sustaining our souls.

The source of this blessing is God the Father and the Lord Jesus Christ. Alec Motyer writes that in this phrase, "the single preposition 'from' governs both names, and has the effect of hyphenating them together into one single source of blessing"[1]. In other words, both the Father and the Son are one. God is spoken of as the Father, showing us the loving parental relationship into which we have been reborn, and the name of the Lord Jesus reminds us of the incredible cost that brought about this relationship. This blessing from the Father's heart comes to us via the death and resurrection of his only Son. Feel the power of it, and then release it to someone else.

Thought

When you greet someone today, say it thoughtfully and even prayerfully.

Prayer

Dear Lord, as I interact with people today, let my words be carriers of grace and peace, lifting and encouraging, and even inspiring those around me.

---

[1] Alec Motyer, *The Message of Philippians,* BST series, (IVP, Leicester, 1984), p.29

DAY SIX

Remembering

Phil.1:3,4

*I thank my God in all my remembrance of you, always in every
prayer of mine for you all making my prayer with joy...*

Paul remembered the look that stole over Lydia's face as she
suddenly understood what he was saying to the little prayer-group
of women by the river bank; (Acts 16:14) he remembered that look
of gratitude on the slave girl's face as she was suddenly freed from the
demonic power that had bound her for years; (Acts 16:18) and he
remembered that look of utter amazement on the gaoler's face as he
suddenly saw the power of God. (Acts 16:29) Each time he prayed for
the church, their faces would drift in front of his gaze. They were
historical reference points in his prayers, because this church in Philippi
had been birthed in a place of prayer, a place of conflict and a place of a
sovereign manifestation of the power of God.

Paul was saying to them, "Every time I think of you, I remember your
faces and your stories, and I thank God for you." There were other faces
that he would remember. He would thank God for all of them, saying,
"...always in every prayer ... for you all ... making my prayer with joy."
There are always good reasons for thanking God for the people around
you.

Paul believed every saint was a personal masterpiece in the making:
the individual was important. Over the years, I have been greatly helped
in my pastoral and theological thinking by Eugene Peterson. He believes
God views every individual as a 'Genesis project' – where God takes a
wrecked and wasted life, living in darkness, and by his Spirit, nurtures
them back into wholeness, divine order and fruitfulness.

We must understand the uniqueness of every individual. Nicholas
Berdyaev wrote:

In a certain sense, every single human soul has more meaning and value than the whole of history with its empires, its wars and revolutions, its blossoming and fading civilisations.[1]

Each individual, when converted to Christ, has within them the same Spirit of the God who created the heavens and the earth. By his Spirit, they have become his children, and he gives them his full attention. In the same way, we need to see others as he sees them. They too are deeply loved by the Father, part of the family, chosen to participate in his plans, and full of unbelievable creative potential.

Eugene Peterson wrote:

...the culture conditions us to approach people and situations as journalists: see the big, exploit the crisis, edit and abridge the commonplace, interview the glamorous. But the Scriptures and our best pastoral traditions train us in a different approach: notice the small, persevere in the commonplace, appreciate the obscure.[2]

In another place, he wrote:

I was aware that birds were in the air and bushes and trees but never paid attention to them. I could name a few... but then I became a bird-watcher. Very quickly, I began to notice many varieties, the different colours, songs, flight patterns...[3]

Thought

When God looks at you, he doesn't see a crowd of faces. He notices you.

Prayer

Father, as you lovingly notice me each day, help me to lovingly notice You in my brothers and sisters around me.

[1] Nicholas Berdyaev, *The Fate of Man in the Modern World,* (University of Michigan Press, 1969), p.12
[2] Eugene Peterson, *Working the Angles,* (Eerdmans, Michigan, 1987), p.149
[3] Ibid, pp.155,156

DAY SEVEN

Starter / Finisher

Phil.1:5,6

...because of your partnership in the gospel from the first day until now. And I am sure of this, that he who began a good work in you will bring it to completion at the day of Jesus Christ.

Paul believed that every saint was a participator in the gospel. Here the corporate terminology is important. Participation with God by necessity involves participation with others in the church and authentic interaction with those in the world.

Firstly, it was a purposeful participation. The word is *koinōnia*, which means 'a joint-participation in a common interest or activity'. It had the idea of 'togetherness in purpose', and it also carried the sense of movement and growth. God has called us together for purpose.

Secondly, it was a practical participation. Their faith touched their pockets, (4:15-18) and they stood out from all others in their faithful support of Paul's ministry. The phrase 'out of sight, out of mind' did not touch them at all.

Thirdly, it was a persevering participation. Paul wrote, "...from the first day until now..." He was, in effect, saying, "You folks have stuck with me through thick and thin." This, then, was no initial burst of support that dried up years later – there was a determined constancy about it.

Paul also believed that every saint was a recipient of the perfecting work of God. He had this conviction that the work that God had started in them, he would bring to a completion. Many are good at starting things but not finishing them. Others, on the other hand, are good at picking up the unfinished, or even damaged attempts by others, and bringing them to a successful conclusion. God is a brilliant starter / finisher. What he commences, he completes.

There are three further thoughts here. Firstly, God always takes the initiative in his work in us. Jesus is always the Author and Finisher of our faith. God is not looking for our good ideas. He actually wants us to fold into, and cooperate with, him in whatever he is doing. In fact, Jesus said of himself, "I can do nothing on my own initiative," (Jn.5:30, NASB) and "I do nothing on my own initiative, but I speak as the Father taught me." (Jn.8:28, NASB)

Secondly, God continues the work in us. The verb is intensive in form and expresses a continuous action. What he started, He will keep working on until completed. He will take pains to keep on putting the finishing touches to your life. J.B. Phillips renders the text this way:

> *I feel sure that the one who has begun his good work in you will go on developing it until the day of Jesus Christ.*

Thirdly, God will finish the work he started in us. The expanded translation of the New Testament by Kenneth Wuest puts it like this:

> *He will bring it to a successful conclusion right up to the day of Jesus Christ.*

The Message puts it this way:

> *There has never been the slightest doubt in my mind that the God who started this great work in you would keep at it and bring it to a flourishing finish on the very day Christ Jesus appears.*

Thought

Is there anything that you have started in God that needs to be completed?

Prayer

Father, I thank you that you will never give up on me. I believe that you will continue the patient rebuilding, reshaping and rescheduling of my life right the way into heaven.

DAY EIGHT

Strong Feelings

Phil.1:7,8

*It is right for me to feel this way about you all, because I hold
you in my heart, for you are all partakers with me of grace,
both in my imprisonment and in the defense and confirmation
of the gospel. For God is my witness, how I yearn for you all
with the affection of Christ Jesus.*

Paul had very strong feelings for the believers in Philippi, and those
feelings were reciprocated. His feelings were not whimsical,
dependent upon a memory or a reminder; rather, these people were
deeply etched into his heart and mind. It was right for him, as their father
in the faith, to think like this. They were his spiritual children. The Greek
phrase has the sense of 'it was right for him to think this way, despite
what others thought'. Here, then, was a shepherd who had high thoughts
of his flock, despite the criticisms of others. Paul was strongly defensive
of them, and rightly so. Paul was picking up the heart of Christ, who is
equally very defensive over his own.

We are too easily affected by what other people say and think about
our fellow believers. Something in us tends to gravitate towards believing
the negatives, and it sours and pollutes our opinion of them. David would
write, "As for the saints in the land, they are the excellent ones, in whom
is all my delight." (Psa.16:3) God grieves over leaders who 'rubbish' their
flock.

There were very good reasons for these feelings. These people were
etched upon his heart. He had both fathered them and nurtured them.
Paul was no hireling, who threw in the towel and ran away when the
pressure was on. These were his spiritual children, and therefore he
expressed parental feelings. They had grown together in the things of
God, experiencing both joy and suffering together. Not only had they
participated in the work of the gospel, they had also participated in
receiving grace in the tough times. They had shared together through
thick and thin. These were not mere spectators of the work of God
through Paul; they had experienced it with him, alongside him, and
because of that, he loved them dearly.

What was the source of the feelings? Paul tells us: it was "the affection of Christ Jesus" – The Greek word here is *splagchnon*, and describes 'the deepest feelings'. It literally describes 'the emotions that turn the stomach'. We find the same word when Jesus looked at the multitude in Matt.9:36. He was "moved with compassion" for them.

There is a wrong sort of professionalism in the church that can plague the pastoral ministry. There is a huge difference between running a church and the building of individual people into the body of Christ. Authentic pastoral ministry involves the care of individual souls. Here, Paul was expressing the very heart of Christ towards his flock. It was a heart attitude, not a pretence of love and affection that does not ring true. People sense whether or not they are truly loved. This love that Paul had for the believers in Philippi was a wild, strong love that reached out to them. Paul was actually desperately homesick for them.

The pastor who, like Paul, holds his people in his heart will find them holding him in their hearts.[1]

Thought

In your desire to see the big picture, don't miss the beauty of an individual soul right before your eyes.

Prayer

Lord, help me to love the ones you love with the same depth of intensity that you do.

---

[1] *Robertson's Word Pictures,* e-sword.net

DAY NINE

Pure and Blameless

Phil.1:10,11

...so that you may approve what is excellent, and so be pure and blameless for the day of Christ, filled with the fruit of righteousness that comes through Jesus Christ, to the glory and praise of God.

Paul had been praying that the love which the Philippian believers had found in Christ might abound and even overflow. He was asking that the love of God which had surged into their hearts might now flow out towards others, but guided by knowledge and discernment.

This growth in love had a number of goals. God's love is always strategic and focused. First, it was so that they would approve those things which were excellent. The Greek word that was used here is *diapherō*, and it meant a 'recognition and selecting of those things which need to be brought or pushed through'. Paul wished them to be able to distinguish between the things that differed from each other; to have an intelligent apprehension of what was right and wrong; of what was good and evil; and what should be rejected and what should be recognised. In other words, he would not have them love and approve all things indiscriminately. Things should be esteemed according to their real value. God's love is wise.

It was also the ability to discern the finer points of Christian conduct. These were the 'differing' things – things that were superior in quality. Some things were ordinary, and some things were excellent. Can I put it this way – there are plenty of *ordinary* Christians and not so many *excellent* Christians. The choice between the two is down to us. There are those who see what they can get away with, and there are those who are quite focused about how they live.

God is looking for 'finely tuned' Christian lives. Paul would write to Timothy, "Now in a great house there are not only vessels of gold and silver but also of wood and clay, some for honourable use, some for dishonourable. Therefore, if anyone cleanses himself from what is dishonourable, he will be a vessel for honourable use, set apart as holy,

33

useful to the master of the house, ready for every good work. So flee youthful passions and pursue righteousness, faith, love, and peace, along with those who call on the Lord from a pure heart." (2.Tim.2:20-22)

Secondly, the result was that of being found "pure and blameless", having sincerity and integrity in readiness for the day of Christ. What day is that? It is the day when you and I will stand before him – either at our death or his return. The first word, "purity", is an 'inner stance'; the second word, "blameless", is an 'outer stance'. In other words, purity of spirit, heart and thought leads to a purity of lifestyle.

The end result was that of being "filled with the fruit of righteousness"; the outworking of that which was within. God works it in; they, and we, work it out. Whatever the seed, so is the fruit. We imbibe the life of Christ by the Spirit, and so we manifest the same. The goal is the glory and praise of God. This has nothing to do with improving our image or expanding our ministry and fame. It has to do with making him famous, ensuring that, in whatever we say or do, the Person and the Name of the Lord is held in high esteem. We must adopt the motto of John the Baptist, who exclaimed of Jesus, "He must increase and I must decrease." (Jn.3:30)

Thought

Whatever we fill our lives with will eventually manifest before others. Whatever choices we make will eventually produce a harvest, either negative or positive.

Prayer

Dear Lord, plead help me to discern between the ordinary and the excellent.

DAY TEN

A Godly View (1)

Phil.1:12,13

I want you to know, brothers, that what has happened to me has really served to advance the gospel, so that it has become known throughout the whole imperial guard and to all the rest that my imprisonment is for Christ.

The letter now changes tack into a piece of personal narrative. Paul was in prison. The believers were concerned that because of this, his ministry had been either curtailed or finished. It seems also that some of Paul's enemies were making capital out of the fact that he had been arrested. Paul wanted to set the record straight. It had begun in Jerusalem where he was falsely arrested, and then there was the shipwreck, and then there was this house arrest in Rome. Behind the events, however, were other factors – divine factors.

Paul's imprisonment, in his view, was in fact for Christ. It was actually a divine appointing. (Acts 9:15 / Acts 21:10-14 / Eph.6:20) There are two kinds of circumstances in life: the ones we create, and the ones that are created for us. In the first, we reap the consequences, and in the second, we choose our reactions. These circumstances were created for Paul. He reacted by not dwelling on the fact of his imprisonment, but on the fruit of it. There was a higher reason and a wider purpose. Although others were seeing a severe restricting of his ministry, God had a higher view. In God's economy, restrictions can actually bring redirection and a fresh impetus. Some of the most powerful writings that have deeply affected the Christian world have come from prison cells.

The phrase "I want you to know" is very emphatic. Paul is anxious to impress on them that what they saw as a setback was actually an advance of the gospel. The word "advance" comes from the Greek word *prokopē,* which means 'to cut before'. It was used of pioneer woodcutters that preceded the regular army, cutting a road through a dense forest into previously untouched areas. Paul was saying that the gospel had not been thwarted, but it was advancing and breaking into areas thought untouchable. The setback actually brought a breakthrough!

Paul's imprisonment brought the gospel to specialist Roman soldiers. The Praetorian Guard was made up of nine thousand handpicked men of the Emperor, divided into nine cohorts. These were Imperial bodyguards, on double pay and a good pension. The general public would not see much of these men, but Paul did. Each day, a different soldier would take it in turn to be chained to Paul, who then found himself with a captive audience of one!

Sometimes, we find it difficult to understand what seem to be setbacks and failures. Yet it is a spiritual maturity that looks for the hand of God, whereas a spiritual immaturity will see only the problems. Alec Motyer writes:

> God rules. The pressures of life are the hands of the Potter who is also our Father; the fires of life are those of the Refiner. He does not abandon the perfecting process to others; nor is he ever, in his sovereign greatness, knocked off course by the malpractice of evil men or by the weakness of good men.[1]

We must learn to look at seeming hindrances to see if actually the hand of God is to be discerned. This choice of view will always be ours. Maybe we have to learn to stop complaining about what is happening to us, and look for ways in which God is causing a furtherance of his kingdom.

Thought

God will always leave the choice of view to us.

Prayer

Father, help me to look at life today through your eternal perspective.

---

[1] Alec Motyer, *The Message of Philippians,* BST series, (IVP, Leicester, 1984), p.65

DAY ELEVEN

A Godly View (2)

Phil.1:14-18

And most of the brothers, having become confident in the Lord by my imprisonment, are much more bold to speak the word without fear. Some indeed preach Christ from envy and rivalry, but others from good will. The latter do it out of love, knowing that I am put here for the defense of the gospel. The former proclaim Christ out of selfish ambition, not sincerely but thinking to afflict me in my imprisonment. What then? Only that in every way, whether in pretense or in truth, Christ is proclaimed, and in that I rejoice. Yes, and I will rejoice...

As we have seen, Paul's imprisonment was somehow linked into the greater purposes of the Lord. It had opened a seam of ministry to the elite Roman guards. It also seems that it had encouraged others. Paul, in verse 13, talked not only of these Praetorian guards, but also of "the rest". By this time, Paul had been in prison about two years, and it had become known to a wider circle of people. They had become aware that this apostle was incarcerated for spreading the Christian message.

We need to realise that what happens to us, and how we respond to it, goes far and wide beyond our immediate circle. We just don't know who is looking on, observing what is happening to us, and taking a reading from how we are handling it. We need to be aware of this.

Paul goes on to say that his experience has actually encouraged the timorous among the believers. Opposition and persecution are tactics of the enemy designed to shut down the voice and activities of the church. The enemy loves to frighten and intimidate us into silence. Seeing how Paul saw it, however, and how he handled it, had the opposite effect of putting fresh courage into those who were somewhat nervous about sharing their faith.

On a different tack, as we look through a window into his prison, we can see the personal growth of the man, and also the growth of the kingdom. As we look out of his window, however, we see strife among some of the believers. It always seems that growth will bring with it criticism and disturbances. One can understand it coming from outside the church, but it is always hard to bear when it seems to come from within the church.

Solomon wrote, "Where there are no oxen, the manger is clean." (Prov.14:4) One preacher said:

There is no milk without manure.

Solomon's basic thrust here is that there are always disturbances, criticisms and mess among the saints whenever God is doing something in the church.

From the text it seemed that their malice was aimed personally at him. Paul wrote that they sought to "afflict" him. (v.17) That word comes from the Greek word *thlipsis*, and it means 'to put under extreme pressure'. It carries a real sense of crowding in on him, jumping up and down upon him, worsening his already difficult situation. Very often, the attacks are indeed personal, aimed directly at the man of God. The phrase can literally mean 'to lay more pressure on him making life even more painful'. If we are in any form of ministry, I'm afraid that this comes with the territory. Therefore, we need to get used to it and make sure that our responses are Christ-like.

Motivation, I have discovered, is everything in the things of the kingdom. For some in the church at Rome, it was envy, rivalry, selfish ambition and pretence that had stirred them up. Maybe Paul had posed a threat to them. They had been there before he arrived, so were they jealous of his successes? Did they personally seek success in order to prove a point? For others, it was good will, love and truth. Christ had filled their hearts, and they were more than glad to work with others. For them, evangelism was an overflow. Paul's big-hearted reaction to those who opposed him is wonderful to note. He felt that however Christ was preached, from whatever motive, he would rejoice. His huge heart was able to rejoice with his critics seeing fruit. There is so much that we can learn from this.

Thought

Rejoice when you personally see success, and learn to rejoice when your critics do as well.

Prayer

Dear Father, give me such a heart that I can rejoice when my critics lead others to Christ.

DAY TWELVE

The Power of Prayer

Phil.1:19,20

...for I know that through your prayers and the help of the Spirit of Jesus Christ this will turn out for my deliverance, as it is my eager expectation and hope that I will not be at all ashamed, but that with full courage now as always Christ will be honored in my body, whether by life or by death.

Paul, as we are seeing, was severely restricted in his movements. Chained to a different seasoned soldier every day, it looked like his apostolic ministry was at an end. But that is not how Paul saw it. He found himself surrounded by individuals – each with his own story, background and temperament.

Paul always saw the bigger picture. He saw that God ordered his circumstances, and he trusted him. Whatever occurred to him, God would see to it that it worked out, not only for his benefit, but for the benefit of those around him. The Weymouth translation of the New Testament puts it this way: "What is happening to me will be for the good of my own soul."

Alec Motyer wrote:

The Christian need never fear the outcome of events.[1]

Because Paul could see God's hand in his life and in the lives of these hardened soldiers, he rejoiced over and over again. In fact, he repeats the fact that he rejoices, in a very determined way. The way that the Greek word *charēsomai* is put together indicates a determination to rejoice in spite of the facts, and in the face of the facts. It was hard, especially when some of the brothers were speaking against him, but, nevertheless, he chose to rejoice. This is spiritual maturity at its best!

Under these circumstances, Paul looked for help from two sources: one was human and the other was divine. Firstly, he looked to his brothers and sisters in the faith, asking them to pray for him. He was

---

[1]   Alec Motyer, *The Message of Philippians,* BST series, (IVP, Leicester, 1984), p.84

never ashamed to ask for prayer. He demonstrated a confidence that when the believers began to pray, things would begin to happen. He used the phrase "I know", and it is the Greek word *eidō*, which is a seeing word – a revelation word. This was not a knowledge gained from a book, or even experienced; it was something he had seen in the Holy Spirit, and it had left an indelible mark on his soul, becoming a reference point in his life.

The second source that Paul looked to was divine. It was the help of the Spirit of Jesus Christ. This was a typically Pauline expression. Paul saw the Holy Spirit as the manifest presence of Christ. Gordon fee wrote that "Christ has put a face on the Holy Spirit"[1]. Augustus Strong wrote that "the Holy Spirit is Christ's alter-ego"[2]. Fee also calls the Holy Spirit "God's empowering presence"[3] and our "constant divine companion"[4]. Paul saw that the prayers of the believers and the work of the Holy Spirit went hand in hand. They were inseparable. This clearly demonstrates the saying of John Wesley: "God does nothing except by answer to prayer." We must never underestimate the power of the church at prayer, and the overflowing, encircling, uplifting, strengthening provision of the Spirit of Jesus Christ.

Thought

God does not want you to struggle through today on your own. Reach out for help.

Prayer

Lord, help me to include myself into the prayers of others, and in so doing, may I sense the encircling and uplifting of the Holy Spirit of Christ today.

---

1   Gordon Fee, *God's Empowering Presence,* (Baker Academic, Michigan, 1994), p.6
2   A.H. Strong, *Systematic Theology,* Vol 1, (Judson Press, 2009)
3   Gordon Fee, *God's Empowering Presence,* (Baker Academic, Michigan, 1994), p.5
4   Ibid, p.53

DAY THIRTEEN

Eager Expectations

Phil.1:20

...as it is my eager expectation and hope that I will not be at all ashamed, but that with full courage now as always Christ will be honored in my body, whether by life or by death.

We are now given another insight into Paul's mind and heart. I'm not sure what we might think if we were in the same position. One thing is for certain, Paul was facing a trial, and the verdict was either going to be life or death. He was to appear before Nero, one of the most unstable emperors Rome had ever known. For most men, the prospects would have filled them with fear.

With Paul, however, the opposite was true. Paul was expecting deliverance. The word he used was *sōtēria*, and is better translated 'salvation'. From the context, however, we can see that he was prepared for the worst. He felt that whichever way the court ruled, he was going to be a winner.

Note his attitude towards the coming court appearance. It was with "eager anticipation". A number of scholars, looking at this unusual word *apokaradokia* (found only here and in Rom.8:19), have concluded that this was probably constructed by Paul himself. It was made up of three words 'away', 'the head' and 'watch', which had all been strung together. It described a person "with head erect and outstretched, whose attention is turned away from all other objects and riveted upon just one"[1]. Paul was earnestly looking forward to his court appearance, or as another writer put it, he was standing "on tiptoe"[2].

Paul expected that at this court appearance he would be given an opportunity to speak unashamedly about his faith, and that Christ would be honoured. For him, the greatest shame would be to let his Master down. Maybe he was thinking of the words of Jesus, who said, "...and when they bring you to trial and deliver you over, do not be anxious

---

[1] Kenneth Wuest, *Word Studies in the Greek New Testament,* Vol.2, (Eerdmans, Michigan, 1973), p.43

[2] J.B. Phillips

beforehand what you are to say, but say whatever is given you in that hour, for it is not you who speak, but the Holy Spirit." (Mk.13:11)

What we do know is that he was thinking of the honour of Christ. He was not bothered about his own fate.

He felt that the prayers of the saints, and the orchestrated help of the Spirit, would bring him to a place of "full courage" ("sufficient courage", NIV) in front of Nero. The word there meant a 'forthrightness in public speaking' or a 'frankness of speech that arises out of a freedom of heart'.

Paul was anxious for the honour of Christ. The way the Greek was constructed, in the passive sense, it was not that Paul would honour Christ, but that Christ would be honoured. The focus was not on Paul himself behaving bravely and well, but on the honour of the Lord Jesus. There is a huge difference between the two. Christ was be honoured, with or without him, whatever the outcome of the trial. This was a pure and unadulterated love of the honour of Christ, and is something to be emulated among us.

Thought

Do not be concerned how you will look in the circumstances that you are walking through; rather be concerned on how Jesus is going to look.

Prayer

Dear Lord, please forgive me for my over-attention to my reputation. Give me a determined passion for yours.

DAY FOURTEEN

Living or Dying (1)

Phil.1:21-24

For to me to live is Christ, and to die is gain. If I am to live in the flesh, that means fruitful labor for me. Yet which I shall choose I cannot tell. I am hard pressed between the two. My desire is to depart and be with Christ, for that is far better. But to remain in the flesh is more necessary on your account.

Paul's eager expectation and hope was that, during his trial, Christ would be honoured whatever happened to him. As we have already mentioned, the word *apokaradokia* was unusual. Kenneth Wuest translates it "my undivided and intense expectation"[1]. Paul was in effect saying, "I am craning my neck, ignoring all else, desiring above all else, whatever happens, the honouring of my Master."

Paul used another word in the mix. This word "hope" was an interesting one. Alec Motyer writes:

> *Christian hope makes the outcome certain but leaves open the time of fulfilment and the means by which the goal is reached.*[2]

Paul's goal in life was the honouring of Christ, but how that was going to be achieved was uncertain. In the previous verses, Paul was decisive; here he was somewhat indecisive.

For Paul, to live was Christ. Life had absolutely no meaning to him apart from Christ. He was not one of those 'weekend Christians'. He lived in and for Jesus Christ twenty-four hours a day. In his letter to the Colossians, he wrote that "Christ is our life". (Col.3:4) Paul was totally absorbed by Christ, who had become everything to him. All previous gain was counted as garbage compared to the surpassing worth of knowing Christ Jesus his Lord. Paul was far more interested in knowing Christ

---

[1] Kenneth Wuest, *The New Testament – an Expanded Translation,* (Eerdmans, Michigan, 1973), p.460

[2] Alec Motyer, *The Message of Philippians,* BST series, (IVP, Leicester, 1984), p.87

personally than in whatever he could achieve for him. Alec Motyer also wrote:

> ...*his whole life may be summed up as the progressing abandonment of everything else in the interest of gaining more and more of Christ.*[1]

The Good News Bible (GNB) puts it this way: "For what is life? To me, it is Christ. Death, then, will bring more."

For Paul, to die was actually gain. This hits hard at the fear of death, the fear of the final unknown. For many, death is the final defeat, the final destination, but that is not how the Christian views it. Death, for a believer, is simply the doorway into heaven. Let us remind ourselves of the words of Jesus, "I am the resurrection and the life. Whoever believes in me, though he die, yet shall he live, and everyone who lives and believes in me shall never die. Do you believe this?" (Jn.11:25,26)

You and I live in a 'win-win' situation.

The word "depart" is *analusai*, and it literally means 'the slipping of a ship's anchor' or 'the striking of a camp'. It is 'the moving on from here'. Death would take Paul into all that he had ever longed for, and the greatest joy for him would be looking into the face of the One he had loved and served.

This is a challenge for us. How much of a grip does this life hold on us? How much of a view of heaven do we have? Which has the greatest influence over our lives? How ready to go are we if heaven called for our immediate presence?

Thought

When we say that Christ is our life, is that a reality or an aspiration?

Prayer

Dear Lord, may my everyday life be so filled with your presence that I will hardly notice the transition from earth into heaven.

---

[1] Ibid, p.87

DAY FIFTEEN

Living or Dying (2)

Phil.1:21-26

For to me to live is Christ, and to die is gain. If I am to live in the flesh, that means fruitful labor for me. Yet which I shall choose I cannot tell. I am hard pressed between the two. My desire is to depart and be with Christ, for that is far better. But to remain in the flesh is more necessary on your account. Convinced of this, I know that I will remain and continue with you all, for your progress and joy in the faith, so that in me you may have ample cause to glory in Christ Jesus, because of my coming to you again.

Paul was eagerly anticipating facing Nero, and of seeing the Lord Jesus honoured. He was not too worried about the outcome of the trial, but his deepest desire was that Jesus was honoured. Facing possible death was not a fearful prospect, but it did present a dilemma. It would be a difficult choice for him to make. He was "hard pressed" between the two. This phrase "hard pressed" (ESV/NASB), "torn between the two" (NIV) is the one Greek word *sunechō*, and it means 'to be held together', like two people, each one holding one of your arms and pulling them in opposite directions so that you cannot move.

Ralph Martin notes that this particular passage was written in broken syntax, demonstrating the agitation of Paul's mind.[1] As he faced these two things, he was deeply moved at the close prospect of seeing his Saviour's face.

It is interesting to note that the little phrase "to die is gain" is better translated 'to have died is gain'. Kenneth Wuest wrote:

The tense denotes, not the act of dying, but the consequences of dying, the state after death.[2]

---

[1] Ralph Martin, *The Epistle of Paul to the Philippians,* (Tyndale Press, London, 1963), p.77

[2] Kenneth Wuest, *Word Studies in the Greek New Testament,* Vol.2, (Eerdmans, Michigan, 1973), p.45

Paul was writing of standing in the immediate presence of Christ, seeing him face to face, and feeling his embrace. I love the way C.S. Lewis put it in his last book of the Narnia series, *The Last Battle*. He wrote:

> *The term is over; the holidays have begun. The dream is ended: This is the morning.*[1]

Paul's reason for living is shown in bold relief. He had faced the possibility of the release of death, and now he faced the possibility of life. We see most clearly here the pure unselfishness of the man. His personal preference was to go and be with Christ, but his sense of pastoral responsibility won the day. To remain alive would be for the sake of the church. His personal desire conflicted against the pastoral responsibility that he felt towards the flock, and Christ in him prevailed. What do I mean by that? Simply this: the Spirit of Jesus is sacrificial in its essence.

Paul was able to set aside his own personal preferences for the sake of others. For him, real ministry was not about how much he was personally fulfilled or how well and freely he exercised his gifts; it was more about how much he could lay down his life and desires for the benefit of others. Later in this letter, Paul would state that his disciple Timothy had the same spirit. He wrote, "I have no one like him, who will be genuinely concerned for your welfare. For they all seek their own interests, not those of Jesus Christ." (2:20,21)

This is the way of Christ, and those of us who are called to follow him will want to walk in the same way. (1.Jn.2:6) Jesus was genuinely oblivious of himself, and fully conscious of his Father and of others. Paul was full of this same spirit, this same attitude. This was a high and ancient calling, and it comes again to us today.

Thought

The way of Christ is totally unselfish, and more conscious of God and others than with oneself.

Prayer

Jesus, please root out of my heart any preoccupation with myself, and fill me with your Spirit.

---

[1] C.S. Lewis, *The Last Battle,* The Complete Chronicles of Narnia, (HarperCollins, London, 1998), p.524

DAY SIXTEEN

Balancing the Talk with the Walk

Phil.1:27

*Only let your manner of life be worthy of the gospel of Christ,
so that whether I come and see you or am absent, I may hear
of you that you are standing firm in one spirit, with one mind
striving side by side for the faith of the gospel...*

Here is a subject that was very close to Paul's heart – the conduct of believers. The way we live either reinforces or undermines our Christian testimony. Paul used the word "only". Alec Motyer wrote:

*The force of the word 'only' is tremendous, as if Paul has said,
'this one thing and this only'.*[1]

Living the life of Christ is so important. Many talk about it – not so many actually live it.

Paul encouraged a conduct that was worthy of the gospel. The phrase "manner of life" (ESV), "conduct" (NIV/NASB) is taken from the one Greek word *politeuomai*. We get our word 'politics' from here. He used this word only here and in Acts 23:1. It literally meant 'to live as a citizen'. The word was in the plural and therefore spoke of the Christian community. As citizens of the kingdom of heaven, their practice was to incarnate the gospel they preached. We should ask ourselves today, what ethos do we communicate to the outside world when we are together?

The word "worthy" is the Greek word *axiōs*, which meant 'to weigh as much'. In other words, their "manner of life" and their words were to balance each other. Their walk was to balance their talk. It is also noteworthy that Paul was anxious that this happened whether he was there or not. One of the most frustrating things for a leader is to observe that in his absence things slip back and standards are not maintained.

Paul also encouraged a unity in the face of opposition. Philippi was a Roman colony, and there had been fierce opposition to the gospel from

---

[1]   Alec Motyer, *The Message of Philippians,* BST series, (IVP, Leicester, 1984), p.92

the authorities. Mindful of this, Paul encouraged a standing together and a walking together at very deep levels. Satanic strategy has always been to 'divide and conquer', and so the believers were encouraged to resist this, and pull together. The phrase is full of meaning and can be literally read 'in one spirit with one soul'. In other words, they were to have the same inner fire, the same thoughts, the same feelings and the same choices. Whatever the enemy threw at them, they were to stand together. I have read of enough battle scenes to know that when the enemy sees individuals deserting the field, discouraging others around them, he knows that the conflict is won. In Roman and medieval warfare, the Roman 'tortoise' and the 'shield wall', that involved the locking together of arms, were almost invincible.

But it was not only a *standing* together, it was also a *striving* together. Their faith was not to be merely about mutual assent, it was about mutual action. It was about movement and taking ground. We get our word 'athletics' from here, but the stress was not on individual prowess, but on team effort. He was saying, "Walk together; push together; run together; strike together." Wuest described it as "an athletic contest in which a group of athletes cooperate as a team, against another team, working in perfect coordination against a common opposition"[1]. We need to make inroads together.

Thought

The balanced Christian life is where talk and walk are evenly matched.

Prayer

Dear Lord, in this culture I live in, that super-elevates personal thinking, help me, with my brothers and sisters, to collectively find the mind of Christ.

---

[1] Kenneth Wuest, *Word Studies in the Greek New Testament,* Vol.2, (Eerdmans, Michigan, 1973), p.52

DAY SEVENTEEN

Facing Fear and Intimidation

Phil.1:28-30

...and not frightened in anything by your opponents. This is a clear sign to them of their destruction, but of your salvation, and that from God. For it has been granted to you that for the sake of Christ you should not only believe in him but also suffer for his sake, engaged in the same conflict that you saw I had and now hear that I still have.

The power of a united army is frightening. Individual ventures are quickly picked out for either seduction or destruction. Any church where the members are in an authentic heart unity with each other presents a serious challenge to the powers of darkness, and any city where there is an authentic heart unity between the churches is seriously bad news for the darkness. Establishing and maintaining this kind of unity, however, is hard graft, easily discouraged, but it is a ground that must be won if we are going to make serious inroads for the kingdom of heaven.

The enemies of this fledgling church were seeking to frighten and intimidate them. Paul used a unique word to describe this, *pturomenoi,* and it meant 'the uncontrollable stampede of startled horses'. In the face of such full frontal, overwhelming and often shocking attacks, Paul was saying, "Hold your ground. Don't be intimidated. Stand firm, and stand firm together. Learn to hold ground, move as a single unit and learn your need of each other. It is together that we rise, and it is together that we should take the knocks. The key word is 'together'. When we stand and operate like this, we actually send a clear signal to the enemy that it is his destruction, and not ours, that is certain."

Here in the West, we know very little of this shocking and terrifying kind of persecution. But it still continues in certain parts of the world today. Our response should be one of identification and prayer for those who are suffering for the cause of Christ. If it happened here, it would shock us, and maybe it would galvanise us into much deeper levels of unity and prayer.

Paul wanted the believers to understand that suffering was actually a gift from God. He wrote, "...it has been granted to you that for the sake of Christ you should not only believe in him but also suffer for his sake..."

We need to get a biblical understanding of this gift of suffering. Just as faith for believing is a gift, so is suffering. Here in the West, we major on the believing aspects of our faith, but we tend to avoid the concept of the suffering aspects of our faith. Paul would later write to Timothy, saying, "Share in suffering as a good soldier of Jesus Christ." (2.Tim.2:3). Later in the same letter, he wrote, "Indeed, all who desire to live a godly life in Christ Jesus will be persecuted." It was not *could be;* it was *will be.* It begs the question then, how godly are we?

It was a suffering for his sake. Marvin Vincent, writing of the believers in Philippi, put it this way:

> *Suffering was the marriage-gift when they were espoused to Christ: the bounty when they enlisted in His service.[1]*

It is said that Thérèse of Lisieux wrote:

> *Suffering is the very best gift He has to give us. He gives it only to His closest friends.[2]*

It is also an engagement into a shared conflict. Paul's struggles had become their struggles. There is much we can learn from this. We must never let our brothers and sisters feel that they struggle alone. Remember also that conflicts within and around us are actually the arena for the growing and strengthening of the spiritual muscles of the soul. Let's not avoid it.

Thought

God has given us three wonderful gifts: salvation, the Spirit and suffering.

Prayer

Please, God, give me a heart that will link with others who are suffering today.

---

[1]   Marvin R. Vincent, *Vincent's Word Studies,* e-sword.net
[2]   Thérèse de Lisieux

50

DAY EIGHTEEN

Encouragement in Christ

Phil.2:1

So if there is any encouragement in Christ, any comfort from love, any participation in the Spirit, any affection and sympathy…

Although most probably Paul's favourite church, we need to remind ourselves that this letter was addressed to a group of people that were suffering not only from persecution and hardships around them, but also from petty divisions from within. (4:2) A favourite strategy of Satan has always been to 'divide and conquer'. Here, Paul was asking them to stand together, firstly, with a unity of heart. When our hearts are not together, there can be no real unity, and that will affect our effectiveness. Then, secondly, they were to stand together with a harmony of hearts. Variety in unity is the Father's design; like an orchestra playing different instruments and different notes, but the same song, the same piece and page of music. We all have different backgrounds, gifts and perspectives, but the goal and direction is one: to be "standing firm in one spirit, with one mind striving together for the faith of the gospel…"[1] God is looking for a unity and harmony at heart level.

We now come to the second chapter, and we find the Greek word *oun*, translated "so". It meant 'in the light of what has just been written'. Incidentally, we can catch a glimpse of the Trinity here in the encouragement of Christ, the love of the Father and the fellowship in the Spirit – together forming the greatest example of unity.

Paul was not questioning the existence of these things; they did exist. The Greek word *ei* is a conditional particle referring to a fulfilled condition. It is better translated 'since'. The question was then, seeing that these things existed among them, like pillars in a building, did they actually affect and move the church into a unity? These four pillars were

---

[1] Philippians 1:27 (NASB)

actually motives for unity; they were grounds for appeal,[1] and they exerted a pressure and an influence, which urged and nudged the believers together.

The first 'pillar' was "encouragement in Christ". The Greek word for "encouragement" is *paraklēsis*. It was full of meaning. It meant 'to call to one's side'. It meant 'to exhort, to lift up, to strengthen'. The sense was that, alone, they would find it difficult to come together. The living Jesus, however, looked upon, studied, imitated and communed with, should become a real source of encouragement to live together in love and unity. Paul was saying that as they walked closely with him, then they would want to walk closely with each other. They needed the Lord, and they needed the Lord in each other.

Likewise, as we walk close to the Master, we will gain an understanding of his heart. The whole basis of his mission was reconciliation. He came to bring you and me and the Father, together. If we seek to imitate him, then our whole thrust of our lives will carry this same heart. This is a great ministry for the body of Christ, and this biblical kind of "encouragement" is always both sympathetic and animating, and it puts 'heart' into people. Let's be doing it!

Thought

Is there someone out there today that I can put heart into? Instead of correcting them, could I confirm something in them?

Prayer

Father, today will you give me the eye of an eagle to spot someone who could do with a living word of upbuilding, encouraging grace?

---

[1]   J. Hugh Michael, *The Epistle of Paul to the Philippians,* (Hodder & Stoughton, London, 1954), p.74

DAY NINETEEN

Comfort and Fellowship

Phil.2:1 (ESV)

So if there is any encouragement in Christ, any comfort from love, any participation in the Spirit, any affection and sympathy...

In Acts 2:42, we find the four basic pillars of church life. "And they devoted themselves to the apostles' teaching and the fellowship, to the breaking of bread and the prayers." Here, Paul gave what I have called 'the four pillars of unity'. If the first pillar of unity was "encouragement in Christ" then the second was "comfort from love". This word "comfort" or "consolation"[1] is the Greek word *paramuthion*. It is only used here in the whole of the New Testament, and it contains within it the two elements of 'tenderness' and 'persuasion'. In classical Greek, Plato used the word to denote 'incentive' and 'stimulant'. It can better be described as 'the gentle, nudging, prodding and melting love of God that gradually and persistently breaks through all cold indifference, hardness and even rebellion'. As it touched these believers, it evoked a response. In the same way, our love for him is only a response to his initiating and persistent love for us. John the apostle would later write, "We love Him because He first loved us." (1.Jn.4:19)

It did not stop there, however. This comforting love of heaven gently and firmly nudged them forward, inwards and outwards, and it sought to express itself through them to others. As they yielded to this wonderful comforting love of the Father, they began to see others as he saw them. This agape love broke down all their prejudices and personal feelings, and wanted to say to them, "See what I see and feel what I feel." The Father, in securing their salvation, came all the way to where they were, and personally removed all the barriers to reconciliation. He initiated the process, and kept it going even when they wanted to back away. God's love pursued them, healed them and broke through them.

The third pillar of unity was what Paul called "participation in the Spirit". The word "fellowship" is that familiar word *koinōnia*, and it

---

[1] e.g. GNB

carried all the ideas of 'fellowship, association, community, communion, joint participation and intimacy'. This is not some kind of religious club that they belonged to; this was a supernatural family that they had been born into. Likewise, for true fellowship, we too must be born again, experiencing a new birth by the power of the Holy Spirit; his Spirit coming to ignite our spirit, with an infilling of a new dynamic that cleanses, refreshes, empowers and envisions us. When the Spirit brings us into this family, God becomes our heavenly Father, Jesus becomes our elder Brother, and we become brothers and sisters. The Holy Spirit takes us by the hands and tells us that we are somehow related.

The ministry of the Spirit was, and still is, to draw God's children closely together, knitting them together, and building up this one body of Christ. It is a difficult work, because we are not naturally inclined to this because of our inborn and natural independence. Ralph Martin wrote:

> This doctrine should sound the death-knell to all factiousness and party spirit.[1]

We were all baptised by one Spirit into one body, and so the Holy Spirit will never lead us into schism or independence. When we are listening to him, cooperating and flowing with him, we will find that we will be getting closer to Christ and closer to each other. We need to let these things touch and nudge us.

Thought

If we meditate much on the unity of the Spirit, we will matter much to each other.

Prayer

Dear Lord, help me to see what you see in my brother or sister's face.

---

[1] Ralph P. Martin, *The Epistle of Paul to the Philippians,* (Tyndale Press, London, 1963), p.91

DAY TWENTY

Affection and Compassion

Phil.2:1

So if there is any encouragement in Christ, any comfort from love, any participation in the Spirit, any affection and sympathy...

We have looked at three pillars of unity – three couplets – and we now come to the fourth. Here, again, Paul used two words. The first word was *splagchna*. Kenneth Wuest translates it "tenderheartednesses". It literally meant 'inner parts' and describes an experience that is felt inwardly.

This was the word frequently used to describe the emotions of Christ on a number of occasions; for example, when he saw the multitudes helpless, lost, hurting and without a shepherd, the Bible says that he was "moved" with compassion. In other words, what he saw got to him. In the same way, when we suddenly see things that are shocking, we feel the same. Our tummy turns with either grief, distress, shock or compassion, and our breathing and heart-rate begin to quicken a little. This, you see, is a 'felt' word. It can either take us by surprise, or we can open up our hearts to let it happen. The opposite emotion is hard-heartedness and cold indifference, and sadly, in our information-drenched world, this can so easily become the norm. We can find ourselves becoming blasé or hardened to so much misery and pain around us, that our hearts and minds become numbed and eventually hardened. Jesus actually allowed what he saw get to him, and perhaps we need to do the same.

In any case, it is my firm conviction that the only valid motive for any kind of ministry is this word *splagchna* – a visceral compassion. All other motives are pretenders.

The second word that Paul used was *oiktirmoi*, which meant 'pity and compassion for others'. It was a word that was outward-looking, and it primarily looked at the plight of others. This 'couplet', then, was quite literally 'root and fruit'. The first was 'felt', the other was 'manifested'. The first was inward; the other was outward. For us today, the first is my brother's plight touching me; the other is me touching my brother's plight. We have to learn how to be emotionally tactile. Words, without heart and emotion, are empty of any power to heal or to lift.

Usually, divisions within the body of Christ bring about the entrenchment and defence of strongly held opinions, feelings and positions. This is followed by a rationalization of the reasons for any breakdown. The other party's feelings then become unseen, isolated and unimportant in the light of our own need to assert that we were in the right. Our defensiveness, in a nutshell, is nothing more than pure and unadulterated selfishness, and it comes, not from the Holy Spirit, but from a more primal survival instinct.

This particular pillar of unity comes to us, nudging us and saying, "I know you are hurting, but so also is your brother or sister. Come out of your own trench and go and sit in his or hers for a while. You might actually see another perspective on it all." Somebody has to make the first move, and we, feeling wronged, inwardly insist that it is not going to be us. In the greatest separation of the cosmos, we do not find it written that God so loved the world that he stayed right where he was. The biblical evidence is clear on this. God, in Christ, stepped out of heaven, searched for us, lived among us and gave himself for us that we might be reconciled to the Father.

Thought

Which is more important to chase? Your vindication or your brother's heart?

Prayer

Dear Holy Spirit, would you please melt my heart today?

DAY TWENTY-ONE

Stances of the Soul

Phil.2:2

...complete my joy by being of the same mind, having the same love, being in full accord and of one mind.

We now move on to another four couplets, and I have called these the four 'stances of the soul'. A stance of the soul is simply a chosen attitude and mindset that is motivated and inspired from the life of Christ within us. It can be shaped by circumstances, but that betrays a spiritual immaturity. It needs to be shaped by the word of God, by fellowship with Christ and by the work of the Holy Spirit.

The context is this nudging work of God in bringing believers together into a deep unity. Paul now clearly outlines what this desire of the Spirit looks like. Although we have spent quite some time on this, it needs to be repeated, reinforced and underlined, because this is such a big issue to the Lord, who prayed "that they may be one even as we are one, I in them and you in me, that they may become perfectly one". (Jn.17:22,23)

The believers in Philippi were Paul's "joy and crown" (4:1) and here, he says to them, "...make my joy complete" (NIV) – literally, 'fill up my joy' – by taking on these four stances of soul.

The first stance was to be "of the same mind". The phrase is to *auto phronēte*, and it literally means 'thinking the same thing'. Have you noticed that we do have this deep desire in the West to guard and cherish our own individuality? Paul, however, is teaching something deeper. He is encouraging the subjecting of our personal thoughts to the mind of Christ.

The second stance was to "[have] the same love". This literally means possessing the same *agapē* love that God has, that Christ has. This goes far, far deeper than our personal preferences, whether they are musical, fashion or even 'people groups'. It is the same love in the sense that whoever touches us touches the same love of Christ. The love of God knows no cliques.

The third stance was to be "in full accord". The phrase is *sunpsuchoi*, which literally means 'soul with soul' or 'souls together'. This word is only found here, and it is quite a powerful statement. Paul is encouraging a 'community psyche or soul', which will entail a community sensation, affection, desire and passion. It is as if the Master breathes and we all sigh.

The fourth stance was to be "of one mind". The Greek phrase is *en phronountes* – literally 'thinking the one thing'. Again, we can almost idolise our own individuality to the point that we miss the richness of community thought and expression. The phrases "we think" and "we feel" need to be heard more often. Paul was not talking about cloning here, but about 'harmonizing'. This happens when we take our different notes and instruments and subject them to the same page of music and the same song. And it is all to do with humility. When he wrote in 1.Cor.2:15 that "we have the mind of Christ", what did that mean? It simply meant that Christ had his own thoughts about situations and people, and the church needed to discover what they were, and then humbly submit their own thoughts to his and then order their day, their words and their worlds around that.

Thought

Remember, your perspective is only that – how you see things. God sees far more than you do.

Prayer

Father, Son and Holy Spirit, breathe your life and vision into me today that I may begin to flow with you in thought and heart.

DAY TWENTY-TWO

Don't Do This

Phil.2:3

Do nothing from selfish ambition or conceit...

Unity in the body of Christ is not automatic. Unity in the church must be worked at, cultivated and preserved. Unity depends on each individual, and it comes about by "effort, obedience and deliberate cultivation"[1]. We are responsible for our own reactions and attitudes. We now come to the part where Paul expands his argument and comes to talk, firstly, about two things we must not do.

Firstly, they, and we, should do nothing from "selfish ambition". The word Paul used was *eritheia*, and it meant 'electioneering or intriguing for office'. It had to do with one's aims in life. J.B. Phillips put it this way: "Never act from motives of rivalry..." Peterson has it, "Don't push your way to the top..."[2] Another commentator translates it as "never acting for private ends". This is all about putting oneself in the foreground, ensuring that we are safe and secure, but neglecting the wellbeing and promotion of others. This attitude is fractious and divisive in its nature and is self-promoting. I believe that it runs counter to the values of the kingdom. It creates strife and leaves wounded people in its trail.

It was written of one of my heroes, Thomas à Kempis, that...

> *...he was modest and retiring both by nature and conviction. He sought no fame or office; silence was his friend, work his companion, prayer his aid, and he was well content to work unknown. His life was outwardly uneventful, and there is little to be told. His main work was the cultivating of the spiritual life and the personal following of Christ; his achievement in this life-work, known in its entirety to God alone, is reflected*

---

[1] Alec Motyer, *The Message of Philippians,* BST series, (IVP, Leicester, 1984), p.105

[2] The Message

in the wide influence and converting power of his 'Imitation of Christ'.[1]

Secondly, they, and we, should do nothing from "conceit". The word Paul used here was *kenodoxia*, which literally meant 'empty glory'. This is a word that is found only here, and it has to do with our assessment of ourselves. J.B. Phillips had it "personal vanity". Self-imposed or sought-after glory is empty. Albert Barnes wrote:

> *...the idea seems to be that of mere self-esteem; a mere desire to honour ourselves, to attract attention, to win praise, to make ourselves uppermost, or foremost, or the main object.[2]*

The NLT puts it this way: "Don't live to make a good impression on others."

Here are some interesting Scriptures: "Do not put yourself forward in the king's presence or stand in the place of the great, for it is better to be told, 'Come up here,' than to be put lower in the presence of a noble." (Prov.25:6,7) Does that sound familiar? Check out Lk.14:8-11. How about another proverb: "Let another praise you, and not your own mouth; a stranger, and not your own lips." (Prov.27:2) And what of this text: "How can you believe, when you receive glory from one another and do not seek the glory that comes from the only God?" (Jn.5:44) The big question here is, where do you want your applause to come from? If you want it to come from others, you could be in danger of losing it from heaven.

Thought

In your heart determine to seek the smile of God first, before and above all others.

Prayer

Father, please shift my gaze away from my own reputation, and fill me with a passion for yours.

---

[1] Leo Sherley-Price, *The Imitation of Christ*, (Penguin Books, London, 1952), p.11
[2] Albert Barnes, *Notes on the Bible*, e-sword.net

DAY TWENTY-THREE

Do This

Phil.2:3

...but in humility count others more significant than yourselves.

After having told the believers what they must not do, Paul continued by telling them what they should do. He wrote that they must first have an attitude of humility. The word he used was *tapeinophrosunē*, and it literally meant 'a lowliness of mind'. The Greek thought of the day, however, regarded this, not as a virtue, but as a curse – a disease that was to be eradicated out of the land. But Paul ennobled this word, making it a virtue instead of something negative. For the Christian, it is a mindset that is quite deliberate, and it results in certain choices being made. It is all about deliberately and sincerely choosing the lower place. Jesus himself said something about this in Lk.14:10.

He then went on to say that they should count others better than themselves. The word "count" or "esteem"[1] is *hēgeomai*, and literally meant 'to be led to a conclusion based, not on feelings, but on carefully weighed facts'. This we can do ourselves, by seriously rehearsing the strengths of others and contemplating our own weaknesses. What a contrast this is to the thinking of this age!

Then, he wrote, they should look to the interests of others. Unfortunately, often it can be our own interests that can dominate conversations. The Christian, however, should take a genuine and sincere concern in the interests of others. It is to be authentically 'self-forgetful'. Let me quote Thomas à Kempis again:

If thou wouldst learn anything of lasting benefit, seek to be unknown and little esteemed of men. For a true knowledge and understanding of himself is a man's highest and most profitable lesson. To account himself as nothing, but always

---

[1] e.g. GNB

to think well and highly of others, is true wisdom and perfection.[1]

Finally, we are to have the mindset of Christ. The Greek phrase that Paul used was *touto phroneite en humin*, and meant 'keep thinking this in you'. The word *phroneite* meant 'to think', and the way and direction of our thoughts are so important. Perhaps the best way to render this is to 'keep thinking the same way that Jesus thinks'. J.B. Phillips actually translates it, "Let Christ Jesus be your example as to what your attitude should be." This is deeper than mere thought processes; this is deeply felt convictions and values that fuel and direct the way we do things. Albert Barnes writes:

The principle in the case is, that we are to make the Lord Jesus our model, and are in all respects to frame our lives, as far as possible, in accordance with this great example. The point here is, that he left a state of inexpressible glory, and took upon him the most humble form of humanity, and performed the most lowly offices, that he might benefit us.[2]

In this life, we can either be humbled or we can choose to humble ourselves. Paul is talking about the latter here. The only ambition that should be found in our heart is to please Christ. (2.Cor.5:9, NASB) All others are imposters and incredibly inferior. Jesus descended in order to lift others high. That was his mindset. This is a great calling, and if we want to closely follow him, then we will adopt the same mindset.

Thought

Don't be so full of yourself and your own things that you cannot see the worth of others.

Prayer

Jesus, grant me the honour of self-forgetful thinking like you do.

---

[1] Thomas à Kempis, *The Imitation of Christ,* Book 1, Chap.2, trans. George Maine (Collins, London,1971), p.35
[2] Albert Barnes, *Notes on the Bible,* e-sword.net

DAY TWENTY-FOUR

Copy Him

Phil.2:6-8

...who, though he was in the form of God, did not count equality with God a thing to be grasped, but emptied himself, by taking the form of a servant, being born in the likeness of men. And being found in human form, he humbled himself by becoming obedient to the point of death, even death on a cross.

There are many scriptures in the New Testament that encourage and exhort us to walk in the way of Christ. The apostle John wrote, "Whoever says he abides in him ought to walk in the same way in which he walked." (1.Jn.2:6) The primary desire of the Holy Spirit is to see Christ formed in us, where he becomes visible in our words, actions and reactions. (Rom.8:29 / Gal.4:19) This passage is one of the most moving and powerful portions of scripture in the whole of the New Testament. All scholars are agreed that they actually formed a hymn or a poem. Here, we see the self-humbling of the king of heaven, who is the model for our lives.

Jesus was the king in the form of God. The word used here was *morphē*, and it expressed 'the outer manifestation of the inner reality'. Jesus was not a god-like man; he was God himself in essence.

Jesus was the king who did not grasp at position. The word used here was *harpagmos*, which meant, among a number of things, according to Bishop Lightfoot, "a treasure to be clutched and guarded against all odds"[1]. J. Hugh Michael noted that J.B. Moffat translated it as "did not snatch..."[2] Positions are jealously seductive.

Jesus was the king who made himself nothing. The NASB has it literally, he "emptied himself". The phrase used was *heauton ekenōse*, and probably the best way to understand this is to say, 'The king changed

---

[1] J.B. Lightfoot, *St. Paul's Epistle to the Philippians,* (Hendrickson Publishers, Massachusetts, 1993), p.?

[2] J. Hugh Michael, *The Epistle of Paul to the Philippians,* (Hodder & Stoughton, London, 1954), p.83

his clothes, and disguised himself, leaving behind his glory, making no use of his powers, and thereby becoming vulnerable.' The change was not a change of 'essence', but a change of 'state'. The Message has it, "He set aside the privileges of deity."

Jesus was the king in the form of a servant. The same word *morphē* is used again here. The king did not clothe himself with humility; he was humility in essence. Jesus was truly the servant king. Humility is part of the divine essence, part of the divine nature. (2.Pet.1:4)

Jesus was the king who took on the frailty of flesh. Two words were used here. The first was *homoiōma*, translated "likeness", which meant 'resembling or similar to', and the second was *schēma*, translated "form", which meant 'that which outwardly strikes the senses'. Here, then, we have a total identification with mankind. God is not flesh and blood, but he clothed himself in human form for our benefit. If you like, 'the king got out of his clothes and put ours on, so that we could smell, see and touch him'. Knox translated it, "He lowered His own dignity."

Jesus is the King who became obedient even to death. True humility always reveals itself in obedience to the will of another. The sentiment 'nobody tells me what to do' is alien to the mind of Christ. Jesus is the king who was crucified. Cicero called crucifixion "the most cruel and frightful means of execution". It is extremely painful and so humiliating. You couldn't get any lower. This was, and still is, the way of Christ.

Thought

Titles and positions are notorious for affecting us in the wrong way. They should have nothing to do with status, but Christ-like function.

Prayer

Dear Father, teach me the grace of descending in order that I might lift others.

DAY TWENTY-FIVE

See Him

Phil.2:9-11

*Therefore God has highly exalted him and bestowed on him
the name that is above every name, so that at the name of Jesus
every knee should bow, in heaven and on earth and under the
earth, and every tongue confess that Jesus Christ is Lord, to
the glory of God the Father.*

After the humbling, we see Jesus the king highly exalted. As a result
of his agreed and chosen humiliation, he was lifted up. This was
the decision of the Father. The Son came to glorify the Father,
and he also came to exalt us to the same height as himself. This exaltation
was not sought but given. And because he gave all, he received all. But
he received it in heaven. Here, on earth, he received acceptance and love
by some, but dishonour and rejection by most. There, in heaven, he
received a crown and a Name. It needs to be said that that humility that
bides it time whilst waiting for exaltation is not true humility, but an
imposter. True humility is in essence unconscious of itself.

The phrase translated "highly exalted" is *huperupsōse*, which meant
'to exalt to and beyond the highest rank and power'. Again, it is a word
that is found only here. There is no higher position.

Jesus is the king with the Name. It was a given name. The Greek word
used was *charizomai*, and it meant 'graciously given'. As the Son
graciously gave himself to us in humiliation, so the Father graciously gave
him a Name. It was also not just *a* name, but *the* Name. Adam Clarke
has written, and I quote in full:

*The man Christ Jesus is exalted to the right hand of God, far
above all principality, and power, and might, and dominion,
and every name that is named, not only in this world, but also
in that which is to come. From which it appears that no
creature of God is so far exalted and so glorious as the man
Christ Jesus, human nature being in him dignified infinitely
beyond the angelic nature; and that this nature has an
authority and pre-eminence which no being, either in heaven*

or earth, enjoys. In a word, as man was in the beginning at the head of all the creatures of God, Jesus Christ, by assuming human nature, suffering and dying in it, has raised it to its pristine state. And this is probably what is here meant by this high exaltation of Christ, and giving him a name which is above every name. But if we refer to any particular epithet, then the name Jesus or Saviour must be that which is intended; as no being either in heaven or earth can possess this name as he who is the Redeemer of the world does, for he is the only Saviour; none has or could redeem us to God but he; and throughout eternity he will ever appear as the sole Saviour of the human race. Hence, before his birth, Gabriel stated that his name should be called Jesus; giving for reason, he shall save his people from their sins. The qualifications of the Saviour of the world were so extraordinary, the redeeming acts so stupendous, and the result of all so glorious both to God and man, that it is impossible to conceive a higher name or title than that of Jesus, or Saviour of the world.[1]

This Name carries incredible authority, and is the highest Name to which we appeal.

Jesus is a king who is to be worshipped and honoured. The reason for the exaltation is the confessing of all tongues, and the bowing of all knees that are found in the heavenly, earthly and demonic realms. This will be either a willing or an enforced confession and bowing.

Someone has written:

> *'What is the way?' they asked Him.*
> *He said, 'I am the way, follow Me.'*
> *'Where are You going?' they asked.*
> *'To that place below all men so that I can lift them up to heaven,' He said.*

May God grant us the grace us to follow in his footsteps.

Thought

The story is told of a church deacon who was given a medal for his humility, and then chided because he wore it to church the following Sunday!

---

[1] Adam Clark, *Commentary on the Bible,* e-sword.net

Prayer

Lord, in my heart, I worship you – the One with the highest Name of all!

DAY TWENTY-SIX

Working It Out

Phil.2:12-13

Therefore, my beloved, as you have always obeyed, so now, not only as in my presence but much more in my absence, work out your own salvation with fear and trembling, for it is God who works in you, both to will and to work for his good pleasure.

Here, as we start this new section, we find the word "therefore", linking the previous comments with what Paul is now about to write. He is therefore saying that the example of Christ's magnificent example of self-humbling and exaltation ought to govern the way we outwork our own faith. He, and not any other, must be the model for our lives.

Firstly, in this passage, we see that there is 'an unwatched obedience'. Paul had written, "...not only in my presence, but much more in my absence..." The book of Chronicles talks of the boy king Joash who "did what was right in the sight of the Lord all the days of Jehoiada the priest". (2.Chron. 24:2) However, when the priest died, it became a very different story. Also, in the book of Judges, we can observe a persistent cycle that whenever the godly leadership died, the people reverted back to their sinful ways. An unmonitored obedience, then, is always the evidence of a genuine relationship with and a love of the Lord. (1.Jn.2:3-5) Sheep, however, do have a tendency to wander. In this letter to the believers in Philippi, Paul was looking for them to stand firm, knowing their natural tendencies to wander. He was looking for them to take responsibility for their own walk with God.

Secondly, we see 'an outworked salvation'. The phrase "work out" is translated from the one Greek word *katergazesthe*, which means 'to carry out to the goal, to bring to an ultimate conclusion and finish'. Salvation is firstly worked in us by the Spirit; and by the same Spirit it then has to be worked out. The divine life which has entered must now be manifested and revealed. Alec Motyer wrote:

Your own salvation is to be understood, not as an objective yet to be reached, but as a possession to be explored and enjoyed even more fully.[1]

It is like being given a mathematical equation, and then seeking to 'work it out'. The theme is one of exploration, enjoyment, development and discovery. It is always my responsibility to take care of and expand my own spiritual life.

Thirdly, we see "God who works in [us]". This is the other side of the coin. My diligence is somehow dependent on the working of God's grace. The word "works" is *energōn*, which means 'to effectively energise'. This word is only used to convey supernatural energy, which is brought about when we learn to co-operate with the Holy Spirit. Elsewhere, Paul wrote of his ministry of maturing believers, saying, "For this I toil, struggling with all His energy that that He powerfully works in me." (Col.1:29) There were some large and powerful words to be found here. Firstly, there was *kopiō*, which meant 'to work to the point of fatigue', and then *agōnizomenos* which meant 'to struggle, to wrestle, to agonise'. Note carefully that this was a divine pressure coming from within, and not a human pressure from without.

The perfect balance is both having faith in, and responding to, God's ability. Faith is responsibility – my response to God's ability. God works his 'will' (literally, 'desire and intention') into us, and also the ability to see it through. Peterson puts it this way in The Message: "That energy is God's energy, an energy deep within you, God himself willing and working at what will give him the most pleasure."

Thought

The gift of salvation has been given – now unravel it and explore it to the limits!

Prayer

Dear Lord, please empower me to outwork that which you have worked in.

---

[1] Alec Motyer, *The Message of Philippians,* BST series, (IVP, Leicester, 1984), p.127

DAY TWENTY-SEVEN

Obliterating the Light

Phil.2:14

Do all things without grumbling or disputing...

Paul was a very practical theologian. He had the believers both astounded in the heights, and also in working it out on the ground. He was so intent that the Christ-life was authentically manifested and worked out in their daily living. He then turned his attention to the one thing that would darken their testimony, namely grumbling. Reading through the Bible, especially the Old Testament, we will quickly see that grumbling was actually one of Israel's greatest shortcomings. It betrayed a lack of faith and trust in God and also in leadership. It was powerfully insidious in its effect, having the power to dishearten, whereas the words of the Spirit put life and faith into people. Grumbling invoked the anger of God.

There were two main words that Paul used in this passage. The first one was "grumbling" (NASB/ESV), "complaining" (NIV). The Greek word was *goggusmōn*, and it meant 'to murmur or to mutter'. It was "a secret and inner debate, or a secret displeasure that was not openly admitted to others"[1]. It was basically 'to inwardly seethe'. Kenneth Wuest wrote:

> *It refers, not to a loud, outspoken dissatisfaction, but to that undertone murmuring which one hears in the lobbies – against men, not against God...[2]*

Other related words are 'grousing, fretting, muttering, complaining, griping, chafing, finding fault'. All of this goes on in the confines of one's own heart and mind, unseen by others, and it can sour an attitude, discolour an atmosphere and corrode a community.

In the *Rule of Saint Benedict*, it is written in the footnotes concerning 'murmuring', that it is "underhand and quickly becomes part of the

---

[1] *Thayer's Greek Definitions,* e-sword.net
[2] Kenneth Wuest, *Word Studies in the Greek New Testament,* Vol.2, (Eerdmans, Michigan, 1973), p.75

'under-life' of a community … in the end it affects the whole spirit of the community. For individuals it becomes increasingly addictive and they develop a corresponding blindness to the harm that they are doing to themselves and to others."[1] For Benedict, external consent was not enough; inner consent was called for.

The other word that Paul used was "disputing" (ESV/NASB), "arguing" (NIV). The Greek word was *dialogismōn*, which literally meant 'dialogues'. The word described "the thinking of a man deliberately within himself"[2]; it was "a deliberating, a questioning, a hesitating, and a doubting about what is true"[3]. The key issue is that it then became vocal. This inner discontent manifests itself in words, framing atmospheres, depressing and disheartening those who are listening.

Our human nature is more prone to complain than to commend, and if it doesn't fit our frame of reference, then we feel that we must make comment, usually in negative tones. Stuart Briscoe wrote:

> *There is no way a professional grumbler can shine. The grumbling has to go before the shining is to start. Argumentative people are no credit to Christ.*[4]

We are called to be light-bearers.

Thought

Seeds of discontentment grow into spheres of negativity. Root them out quickly.

Prayer

Lord, help me, not to reason with myself, but to talk over everything with you.

---

[1] Patrick Barry OSB, *The Rule of St Benedict,* Chap.23, (Paulist Press; 2nd ed. edition (1 Sept. 2004), p.18
[2] *Thayer's Greek Definitions,* e-sword.net
[3] Ibid.
[4] Stuart Briscoe, *Bound for Joy,* (Regal Books, California, 1975), p.79

Day Twenty-Eight

Becoming the Light

Phil.2:15-16

...that you may be blameless and innocent, children of God without blemish in the midst of a crooked and twisted generation, among whom you shine as lights in the world, holding fast to the word of life, so that in the day of Christ I may be proud that I did not run in vain or labor in vain.

Whenever we inwardly grumble, murmur and question the things that are being asked of us, it begins to darken the light that we are actually called to be. Paul says that this is not the right way, and we must cease from it "so that" we may shine brightly. Grumbling darkens the light within us and can go on to darken the spirit of the community in which we live. The opposite attitude to grumbling is that of a thankful spirit. Paul wrote in 1.Thess.5:18, "In everything give thanks, for this is God's will for you in Christ Jesus," and again in Eph.5:20, he wrote, "...always giving thanks for all things." How we are, and how we react in adverse circumstances, reveals more about us than anything else. A reluctant obedience does not bless, but it betrays something else.

Paul taught that a willing and happy obedience, even contrary to their personal desires, preferences and personal 'life maps', actually caused the believers to shine in stark contrast to those who walked in, and lived according to, the darkness.

He went on to give three characteristics of this 'shining'. The first one was that the believers were to show themselves to be "blameless". This word, *amemptoi*, described 'those deserving of no censure, and free from fault or defect'. This blamelessness was not only in the sight of God, but also in the sight of others. In other words, this was the establishing of a good reputation. It was about having favour, not only with God, but also with other people. (Acts 2:47 / 24:16) Was it important what others thought of the believers? In some cases, the answer was no, but in this case, the answer was undoubtedly yes. As ambassadors for Christ, their reputation – that which others say about them – determined their credibility.

The next word Paul used was "innocent". This word, *akeraios*, described that which was 'unmixed, pure and not corrupted'. This word spoke of a transparent and visible integrity. Here, there were no hidden areas of darkness, or hidden agendas. Today, we would describe it as being 'as clean as a whistle'. Jesus would actually say of Satan, the enemy, "He has nothing on me."[1]

Paul then used the phrase "without blemish". This word, *amōma*, described a moral, ethical and a social integrity. It described a keeping of promises that had been made; it meant being true to one's word and being absolutely trustworthy in all things. It was actually written of the prophet Daniel that his enemies could not find one single charge to put against him. The biblical record said, "They could find no ground of accusation or evidence of corruption, insomuch as he was faithful, and no negligence or corruption was found in him." (Dan.6:4)

J.B. Phillips rendered Rom.12:17 this way: "See that your public behaviour is above criticism." A good reputation is never conferred; it is earnt, and mostly in the sight of those around us. As followers of Christ, we are meant to be attractively different. When our words and attitudes are incongruent with our actions, then we do not stand out as being attractive or different. Paul taught that there must be something consistently and beautifully different about us – the same difference that light has from the darkness.

Thought

Look at the character of the light in Psa.112:4: gracious, merciful and righteous.

Prayer

Dear Father, may my inner life within be beautifully congruent with my outer life.

---

[1]   John 14:30 (MSG)

DAY TWENTY-NINE

Light in the World

Phil.2:14-17

Do all things without grumbling or disputing, that you may be blameless and innocent, children of God without blemish in the midst of a crooked and twisted generation, among whom you shine as lights in the world, holding fast to the word of life, so that in the day of Christ I may be proud that I did not run in vain or labor in vain. Even if I am to be poured out as a drink offering upon the sacrificial offering of your faith, I am glad and rejoice with you all.

I want to stay with this passage just a little longer. If the role of the believer is to be that of a shining and blazing light, then the setting of the believer must be *in* the world, and not removed from it. God has called very few people to be 'full-time' working within church walls. The vast majority of his people are called to be living and working in the thick of secular society. Their role is to be highly visible as lighthouses, as light-givers. One of the difficulties of being 'full-time' in church work is that we can become 'cloistered' away from the cut and thrust of life on the street. So often our friends are our colleagues, and we can easily lose touch with our neighbours around us. Those who attend church become 'them', and the team becomes 'us'.

In the Sermon on the Mount, Jesus talked about the disciples being the light of the world. They were not to be hidden, but openly displayed for all to see. The truth is that we are the first glimpse the world gets of Jesus Christ.

Note in the passage the contrast between the world and the children of God. Paul describes the world, using language from Deut. 32:5, that they are "a crooked and twisted generation". Unfortunately, as time goes on, mankind does not change for the better. The world as we know it, even today, is "crooked" in that it naturally turns away from the path of truth. Here, Paul used the word *skolios*, an old word meaning 'curved'. Like a bowling ball with an offset bias, it always curves from a straight

74

path. The world is also "perverse"[1] in that it has become 'distorted'. Paul used here the word *diastrephō*, which meant 'to distort, to twist, to turn to one side'. When we keep turning away, we become warped of soul, and our view of life is distorted. The world, untouched by the restorative grace of God, cannot walk a true, straight path. An authentic Christian, however, walking in the light, will eventually clash and become out of sync with the direction the world is taking.

The light of heaven is demonstrated by good works, done in a certain way. Jesus told his disciples, "Let your light shine before men in such a way that they may see your good works, and glorify your Father who is in heaven." (Matt.5:16) Their deeds were to draw attention to the Lord. The light was also demonstrated by the word of life, "held fast" (NASB) and "held out" (NIV). Both truths were present in the phrase, but one came out of the other. Before they could hold it out to others, they needed to hold it fast in their own hearts. Likewise, the word of God is always to be lived out before it is spoken out. It is that which will give credibility to our shining. The incarnated word is powerful in effect.

Our attitude in life will either enhance or detract from our witness. Do we grumble about everything, or do we give thanks in all things? We are called to be blazing lights, light-givers, wherever we find ourselves. Keep the lamp of your heart clean. Walk out of your house today into your world – your mission field.

Thought

We can either be a breath of fresh air or we can bring a stink. It is always our choice.

Prayer

Dear Lord, as I step out into my world today, may I carry with me the sweet life-giving fragrance of Christ.

---

[1] e.g. KJV

DAY THIRTY

The Responsibility of Teachers

Phil.2:15-18

...that you may be blameless and innocent, children of God without blemish in the midst of a crooked and twisted generation, among whom you shine as lights in the world, holding fast to the word of life, so that in the day of Christ I may be proud that I did not run in vain or labor in vain. Even if I am to be poured out as a drink offering upon the sacrificial offering of your faith, I am glad and rejoice with you all. Likewise you also should be glad and rejoice with me.

Paul taught that a grumbling and complaining attitude darkens the testimony to Christ, whereas a thankful and joyful attitude lightens up and enhances the testimony to Christ. Our attitude, therefore, and our mindset is absolutely everything.

The phrase "in the midst" was quite significant. The believers had been saved and called out of their world, and then sent into the very same world that was under the rule of the evil one. (1.Jn.5:19) In the sense of being not of this world, Paul, when he said that they should not be of this world, meant that that they were no longer to live according to its various standards, cultures and paradigms. He wrote to the believers in Rome, "Don't let the world squeeze you into its own mould, but let God re-mould your minds from within..." (Rom.12:2, J.B. Phillips) The Message puts it this way: "Don't become so well-adjusted to your culture that you fit into it without even thinking..." James, the half-brother of Jesus, was very strong: "Do you not know that friendship with the world is enmity with God? Therefore whoever wishes to be a friend of the world makes himself an enemy of God." (Jas.4:4)

We are called to be in the world, but there is a tension that we must learn to live with. We could call it 'a pilgrim mentality'. We live here, but somehow don't belong here. A helpful sailing analogy here is that boats are specifically designed to be at sea, sailing in the waters. If, however, the boat springs a leak, and the sea start to get in the boat, the boat will sink. We are meant to be in the world, but if the world gets inside of us, we will sink, and our testimony will disappear out of sight. (1.Jn.2:15-17)

The phrase "the word of life" is a beautiful phrase, because that is exactly what God's word is. It is "living and active" (Heb.4:12) in itself, and it imparts life to all who receive it and who live in and by it. It is a word that is to be held tight and also to be held out. Alec Motyer wrote:

> *The light of Christian character is an un-interpreted parable if we do not speak about Christ. Equally, speaking about Christ is futile if our lives do not back up what we say.*[1]

Paul was anxious that all his work with these believers would not have been in vain. He had poured out his life for their sakes. This is what true and authentic ministry is. To the Thessalonians he would write, "We were ready to share with you not only the gospel of God but also our own selves, because you had become very dear to us." (1.Thess.2:8) Paul was not constructing his own ministry; instead, he was constructing the church. He was not building up his own platform; instead, he was building up the saints. He literally poured his life into them.

Indeed, he foresaw the day coming when his own lifeblood would be poured out; even that would become a fragrant offering to God. He wrote to Timothy, "For I am already being poured out as a drink offering, and the time of my departure has come. I have fought the good fight, I have finished the race, I have kept the faith." (2.Tim.4:6) We need to recover the willingness to offer ourselves, to abandon ourselves in sacrificial ministry for others. Just like Paul. Just like Jesus.

Thought

Whom and what are you pouring yourself into? There is something beautiful about a poured-out life.

Prayer

Jesus, you poured yourself out for me; help me to follow suit for you and others.

---

[1]   Alec Motyer, *The Message of Philippians,* BST series, (IVP, Leicester, 1984), p.134

DAY THIRTY-ONE

Timothy (1)

Phil.2:19-24

I hope in the Lord Jesus to send Timothy to you soon, so that I too may be cheered by news of you. For I have no one like him, who will be genuinely concerned for your welfare. For they all seek their own interests, not those of Jesus Christ. But you know Timothy's proven worth, how as a son with a father he has served with me in the gospel. I hope therefore to send him just as soon as I see how it will go with me, and I trust in the Lord that shortly I myself will come also.

In this chapter, there are four important characters: Jesus, Paul, Timothy and Epaphroditus. The Christian faith is not all about knowing and holding to propositional truths; it is about the life of God being worked out and exhibited in us. Both are necessary, but one must flow out of the other if it is to be authentic. We need to know and believe truth, but the truth must be outworked and incarnated in order for it to be believable.

The first character is the Lord Jesus, who is the Christian's model. The other three are model Christians. We model our lives on both.

The second character is Paul, who wrote to the believers at Corinth, "Be imitators of me as I am of Christ." (1.Cor.11:1) To the Thessalonians he wrote, "...and you became imitators of us and of the Lord." (1.Thess.1:6) The writer to the Hebrews encouraged the believers to become "imitators of those who through faith and patience inherit the promises". (Heb.6:12) It is our lives, our hearts and our attitudes that are read by others, not the words that we speak, nor the deeds that we perform. The way we live communicates far more than what we say.

Our faith is, therefore, not only something believed, but something modelled. All four have this one thing in common: they poured themselves out for others. This is the way of Christ: "The good shepherd lays down his life for the sheep." (Jn.10:11)

The other two were both key workers that Paul sent to the church in Philippi, so that they could report back to him on how they were all doing. Co-workers are an important feature in the life of the church. We are never called to work in isolation, but together in the community of a team. Much can be said about the dynamics of team. I have seen in church life that it is disposition and attitude, not so much ability, that makes for a good team. If the heart is right, then gifts and abilities can be nurtured.

The first co-worker Paul mentioned was Timothy. We will spend some time looking at him. From the scriptures we learn firstly about his upbringing. In Acts 16:1, we understand that his mother was Jewish and his father was Greek. Then, in 2.Tim.3:15, we see that from an early age he was taught the Scriptures. The term used is the "sacred writings" – *hiera grammata*. Paul was probably referring to the body of teaching that arose out of the Scriptures, which would have been at that time the Old Testament. Timothy's education would have paved the way for his salvation, and so when Paul preached the gospel, Timothy's heart and mind were a well-prepared ground. What an incentive this is to those of us who are parents!

Timothy was then nourished and trained in the words of the faith, and in sound doctrine (1.Tim.4:6), and he was encouraged to continue in it. (1.Tim.4:13-15) Constant exposure to the Scriptures, diligent meditative reading and study of the Scripture will beget and deepen faith. The first Psalm talks of one whose "delight is in the law of the LORD, and on his law he meditates day and night." The fruit from that attentiveness to the Scriptures is that "he is like a tree planted by streams of water that yields its fruit in its season, and its leaf does not wither. In all that he does, he prospers."

Thought

What is your daily diet? What do you feed on? Never underestimate the nourishing power of the Scriptures.

Prayer

Lord, "open my eyes that I may behold wonderful things from your words". (Psa.119:18)

DAY THIRTY-TWO

Timothy (2)

Phil.2:19-24

I hope in the Lord Jesus to send Timothy to you soon, so that I too may be cheered by news of you. For I have no one like him, who will be genuinely concerned for your welfare. For they all seek their own interests, not those of Jesus Christ. But you know Timothy's proven worth, how as a son with a father he has served with me in the gospel. I hope therefore to send him just as soon as I see how it will go with me, and I trust in the Lord that shortly I myself will come also.

We continue to look at Timothy. In 2.Tim.1:5, we learn that his faith was a sincere faith. Paul wrote to him, saying, "I am reminded of your sincere faith, a faith that dwelt first in your grandmother Lois and your mother Eunice and now, I am sure, dwells in you as well." The words translated "sincere faith" are *tēs anupokritou pisteōs*, which meant 'an un-pretended or undisguised faith'. Timothy's faith, as well as that of his mother, Eunice, and his grandmother, Lois, was the real thing. It rang true with authenticity.

Paul had won Timothy to Christ, and in that sense, he had become his spiritual father. He wrote, "...as a son with a father he has served with me in the gospel." There are, in fact, some very endearing terms that Paul used to describe him: "My beloved and faithful child in the Lord..." (1.Cor.4:17), "My true child in the faith..." (1.Tim.1:2), "My beloved child..." (2.Tim.1:2). Fathers in God are a rare breed. To personally lead someone to Christ, and then to nurture them into maturity, is an unbelievably precious honour.

Not only did Paul become his father, he also became his mentor in the things of God. He wrote to him, "You, however, have followed my teaching, my conduct, my aim in life, my faith, my patience, my love, my steadfastness, my persecutions and sufferings that happened to me at Antioch, at Iconium, and at Lystra – which persecutions I endured; yet from them all the Lord rescued me." (2.Tim.3:10,11) The Greek word *parakoloutheō*, translated "follow", carried the sense of 'following closely, always at one's side, always attentive'. This spoke of quality 'one on one' time, which is always so productive in the spiritual formation of individuals.

Also, in Acts 16:2, we read that he was "well spoken of" by the brothers. Paul used the word *emartureōito*, which meant that he had a good reputation, witnessed by significant others. His good character was noticeable. I love The Message's rendition: "Friends in Lystra and Iconium all said what a fine young man he was." This kind of reputation is earnt over time. "If God has called a man for the work, signs of it will be manifest to others."[1]

Yet Timothy was a timid young man, (1.Tim.4:12) and not of a strong disposition. Paul, in writing to the Corinthian church, urged them in saying, "When Timothy comes, see that you put him at ease among you, for he is doing the work of the Lord, as I am. Let no one despise him. Help him on his way in peace." (1.Cor.16:10) In 1.Tim.5:23, Paul encouraged him to "use a little wine for the sake of your stomach and your frequent ailments". In another letter to him, Paul wrote, "I remind you to fan into flame the gift of God, which is in you through the laying on of my hands, for God gave us a spirit not of fear but of power and love and self-control." (2.Tim.1:6,7) One commentator writes of Timothy's "training under females, his constitutional infirmity, susceptible soft temperament, amativeness, and sensitiveness even to tears"[2]. One gets the impression of quite a timid servant of God, but through whose weaknesses God would actually show his strength.

Thought

Bravado is quite empty, but admitted weakness is a receptor for the power of God.

Prayer

Lord, while others are boasting of their strengths, show me the worth of my weaknesses.

---

[1] *Robertson's Word Pictures,* e-sword.net
[2] *Fausset's Bible Dictionary,* e-sword.net

DAY THIRTY-THREE

Timothy (3)

Phil.2:19-24

I hope in the Lord Jesus to send Timothy to you soon, so that I too may be cheered by news of you. For I have no one like him, who will be genuinely concerned for your welfare. For they all seek their own interests, not those of Jesus Christ. But you know Timothy's proven worth, how as a son with a father he has served with me in the gospel. I hope therefore to send him just as soon as I see how it will go with me, and I trust in the Lord that shortly I myself will come also.

Timothy was publicly ordained into the ministry. (1.Tim.1:18 / 4:14 / 2.Tim.1:6) We are not sure where it took place, but as the elders prayed, there was an authority conferred upon him, and there were prophetic words given to him, with which he was encouraged to fight the spiritual battles that he would encounter. There was a gift given and imparted to him. Such times in the church are important.

Paul was not really concerned about his own set of circumstances; he was more concerned about the churches that he was involved with. In 2.Cor.11:28, he writes about his "anxiety for all the churches". What would encourage him would be to hear good news, especially from this young church in Philippi.

Timothy was of "a kindred spirit" with Paul in this. Paul actually said, "I have no one like him." The word is *isopsuchos*, which means 'one in soul' or 'one of equal soul'. It only occurs here in the New Testament. Timothy mirrored all that Paul thought and felt and did. The tragedy was that, of all the people who had worked with him, Paul felt that the only one who was 'one with him' was Timothy. The Greek word *oudeis* is literally 'not even one'. All the others had their own agendas.

Some people have 'mirror minds' in that they see only reflections of themselves. They are more concerned with things like image, success and appreciation. Both Paul and Timothy had 'window minds' in that they were able to look out and see others. Their view on life was objective in that they looked for opportunities to serve, whereas the others had subjective mindsets, interpreting all things in relationship to themselves.

Paul and Timothy shared the same mindset as Jesus, who was genuinely concerned for the welfare of others.

Paul also wrote that Timothy had "proven worth". It was known by the other believers. They knew for themselves, and by experience, the worth of the man. People had watched him, and had had dealings with him, and had come to the settled conclusion that he was a good man.

Timothy had served the Lord alongside Paul. The relationship between them, however, was very much a father and son relationship. Not only did Timothy love Christ; he loved Paul and served him. Not only did Timothy obey Christ; he also obeyed Paul.

We serve the Lord by serving those who lead us, and also by serving each other. Jesus himself said that as we serve those who are "the least" among us, we are actually serving him. Our service for the Lord is always authenticated by our service for others, and our service for others is reflective of our service for God. Thomas à Kempis wrote:

> It is a very great thing to obey, to live under a superior, and not to be one's own master … Go where you may, you will find no rest except in humble obedience to the rule of authority. Dreams of happiness expected from change and different places have deceived many.[1]

Thought

If you want to grow spiritually, find someone to love, serve and obey.

Prayer

Lord Jesus, deliver me from wanting to become the master of my own destiny. I surrendered this when I really started to follow you.

---

[1] Thomas à Kempis, *The Imitation of Christ,* Book One, (Hendrickson, Massachusetts, 2004), p.9

DAY THIRTY-FOUR

Epaphroditus (1)

Phil.2:25-30

I have thought it necessary to send to you Epaphroditus my brother and fellow worker and fellow soldier, and your messenger and minister to my need, for he has been longing for you all and has been distressed because you heard that he was ill. Indeed he was ill, near to death. But God had mercy on him, and not only on him but on me also, lest I should have sorrow upon sorrow. I am the more eager to send him, therefore, that you may rejoice at seeing him again, and that I may be less anxious. So receive him in the Lord with all joy, and honor such men, for he nearly died for the work of Christ, risking his life to complete what was lacking in your service to me.

We now come to another character in this chapter, Epaphroditus. Not a lot is known about his background. In the church, even today, there are a lot of unknown heroes, known and commented upon only by God. We know that he was a Macedonian leader in the church at Philippi, and had been sent by the leadership to Rome, to carry a gift from the church for the imprisoned apostle. (Phil.4:14-18) His name meant 'devoted to Aphrodite (Venus)' and carries the sense of 'charming' or 'lovely'. The name corresponds to the Latin 'Venustus' (handsome) and was a very common name in the Roman period. With Epaphroditus, God turned the pagan background to his name around to denote a lovely Christian, who would reflect the beauty and kindness of Christ.

Paul used three words to describe him, and according to Bishop Lightfoot, the first three words – brother, companion and fellow-soldier – are arranged in both an ascending and deepening scale: "common sympathy, common work, common danger and toil and suffering"[1].

---

[1] Bishop Joseph Lightfoot, cited by John F. Walvoord, *Philippians*, (Moody Press, Chicago, 1971), pp.71,72

Paul first calls him "my brother" (common sympathy). The word here is *adelphos*, and it meant 'from the same womb'. Here was a wonderful mystery: Paul was born a thoroughbred aristocratic Jew, and Epaphroditus was of a thoroughly Gentile background. The same womb, then, was a spiritual one. The Bible teaches us that there is now no Jew or Gentile in Christ, but a new creation, a new man, a new family. Each of us, coming from our totally different backgrounds, actually find ourselves becoming family – kin – through the new birth. We find that we all have a common origin. The Christian faith breaks down all national, cultural and class barriers. In Christ we all come from the same womb.

Secondly, Paul calls him "my fellow-worker" (common work). The word here is *sunergos*, meaning 'working together'. It can be translated, 'a companion in work'. Here, then, is a friendship in the work of God, and hard work done with friends. The sense is that they worked together in a deep harmony. This cannot be achieved by a single note played on a solitary instrument. Epaphroditus was much more than a colleague to Paul; he was a companion, a friend – someone whom Paul wanted to have around him.

Thirdly, Paul calls him his "fellow soldier" (common danger). The word here is *sustratiōtēs*, which literally meant soldiers 'that lived under canvas and fought on the battlefront together'. He was a warrior, out there on the front line, enduring the hardships of temporary accommodation – not someone on defensive guard duty. When Paul went out on spiritual excursions to the front line, Epaphroditus was found with him. Someone has translated this as "being bound together in the same conflict". They were involved together in the same battles, they fought together, and they fought real battles. I believe that it is in 'shared conflicts' that we can actually feel the strengths and the weaknesses of each other. Paul certainly felt the strength of this friend.

Thought

Am I a 'fair weather' friend, or am I a friend 'through thick and thin'?

Prayer

Lord, make me a good friend to have around today.

DAY THIRTY-FIVE

Epaphroditus (2)

Phil.2:25-30

I have thought it necessary to send to you Epaphroditus my brother and fellow worker and fellow soldier, and your messenger and minister to my need, for he has been longing for you all and has been distressed because you heard that he was ill. Indeed he was ill, near to death. But God had mercy on him, and not only on him but on me also, lest I should have sorrow upon sorrow. I am the more eager to send him, therefore, that you may rejoice at seeing him again, and that I may be less anxious. So receive him in the Lord with all joy, and honor such men, for he nearly died for the work of Christ, risking his life to complete what was lacking in your service to me.

L et's stay with Epaphroditus a little longer. In his relationship to Paul, he was a fellow brother, a fellow worker and a fellow soldier. We need to reiterate that life and ministry in God is not designed to be worked out in an individualistic isolation. Whatever we do, it must be on the 'same page', and in relationship with those around us. Good questions to ask ourselves are, 'What am I doing that is contributing to the overall vision?' and, 'Is what I am doing contributing to the overall vision?' In relation to the church at Philippi, however, Paul had other words to describe him.

Firstly, Paul said that he was "your messenger" – the word that he used here was *apostolon*, and meant 'a sent one – an apostle'. Note that he was not *a* messenger, but *your* messenger. He was in relationship with the church in Philippi and was sent by that church. There is an authority that is inherent in being sent. There was no personal agenda with this man; he was at the disposal of others. That is a good place to be, in my view.

Secondly, Paul called him "your minister". The word here was *leitourgon*, and carried the meaning of a 'public servant', the same word used to describe the role of a servant in the public temple worship. The work of God, whatever it is for us, is both sacred and public. The service that Epaphroditus gave to Paul was felt and received as being sacred. I feel it would have involved, not only the sharing of the word of God and the monetary gift with him, but also of the washing of his wounds and most probably doing his laundry! All these things were, and still are, sacred in the sight of God. Word-sharing, money-giving, foot-washing, mundane chores are all sacred ways of serving, because the bottom line is that in doing these things to each other, we are doing them to Christ.

There were two other features about him that are worth mentioning. Paul continues that Epaphroditus was quite sensitive to the feelings of others. He had become desperately ill himself, yet was distressed over the anxiety being felt by his home church. He was more concerned about their feelings than about his own sickness. The word translated "distressed" is *adēmoneō*, the same word used to describe the torment of Jesus in the garden of Gethsemane. It expressed 'being worn out, saturated and overpowered with a heavy grief'. How this man loved his church!

Paul also said that Epaphroditus was sacrificial in his service to others. The phrase "risking his life" is an interesting term. It was, in fact, a gambling term. Older manuscripts used the term "hazarding"[1]. In other words, Epaphroditus recklessly risked his life for Paul's sake. The brotherhoods of the ancient Church, who cared for the sick at the risk of their lives, were called the *parabolani*, or 'the reckless persons'. There was a distinct lack of self-preservation about Epaphroditus. He was not stupid, or unwise, but neither was he was earthbound in his thinking. Epaphroditus was one of those illustrious ones who "loved not their lives unto death". (Rev.12:11) How this man loved his brother!

Thought

"This is the very best way to love. Put your life on the line for your friends." (Jn.15:13, The Message)

Prayer

Dear God, help me to see you in those I work with today, and show me ways that I can serve you in serving them.

---

[1] e.g. ASV

DAY THIRTY-SIX

Epaphroditus (3)

Phil.2:25-30

I have thought it necessary to send to you Epaphroditus my brother and fellow worker and fellow soldier, and your messenger and minister to my need, for he has been longing for you all and has been distressed because you heard that he was ill. Indeed he was ill, near to death. But God had mercy on him, and not only on him but on me also, lest I should have sorrow upon sorrow. I am the more eager to send him, therefore, that you may rejoice at seeing him again, and that I may be less anxious. So receive him in the Lord with all joy, and honor such men, for he nearly died for the work of Christ, risking his life to complete what was lacking in your service to me.

This extraordinary and little-known servant of Christ had been sent by the church at Philippi with a gift to Paul, and also to *become* a gift to Paul. His ministry to Paul was both sacred and official.

This ministry came at a deep personal cost to Epaphroditus, who became seriously ill. Paul twice commented that he had drawn near to death. We don't know what the violent illness was, but we can be fairly sure that it was within the context of loving and sacrificial service to Paul. Life on this earth meant little compared to the joy of serving Christ. Paul, when others were trying to dissuade him from going to Jerusalem and certain death in another situation, cried out, "What are you doing, weeping and breaking my heart? For I am ready not only to be imprisoned but even to die in Jerusalem for the name of the Lord Jesus." (Acts 21:13) There, you saw his heart.

Paul was now sending Epaphroditus back to the church, and here, a different word for "sent" was being used. It was *pempō*, a more general word than that of an 'apostle'. A better translation would be 'despatched'. Not only had Epaphroditus become distressed for the church back home, but Paul had become anxious for the church. He used the word *alupoteros*, meaning 'more without grief'. So, Paul released him from his duties, for their sakes. As A.T. Robertson wrote, this was a "beautiful expression of Paul's feelings for the Philippians and for Epaphroditus"[1].

In conclusion to this remarkable chapter, I want to emphasise a few things. God calls us to work together, in tandem, in harmony. We are not designed to be a bunch of individuals doing our own thing for the Lord. Authentic team relationships happen when, firstly, we put the needs of others above our own personal needs. Secondly, they happen when we put ourselves at the disposal of others, instead of pushing for our own ministry to be recognised and released. Finally, they happen when we realise that it is not our abilities, but our disposition, that counts the most in team dynamics.

The most used Greek word for "kindness" is *chrēstotēs*. The yoke of Christ that he wants to lay on us, the sort that does not chafe or bruise, is called *chrēstos*. Mellowed wine has been called *chriō*, most probably from the root word *chraomai*, which means, among other things, 'a light touch'. This describes a quality that makes us easy to work with. One Greek lexicon calls this quality a "'useful kindness', referring to meeting real needs, in God's way, in His timing or fashion"[2]. There are some people who, although highly gifted and capable, are difficult to work with. It has nothing at all to do with their skills or even their 'anointing' – it has much more to do with their disposition. A kindly or gentle person is a joy to work with. There is a softness in the tone of voice; there is a pliability in the disposition, an adaptability to others and circumstances, and a willingness to fold in with others. May God so work in us that we, too, become a delight to work with!

Thought

Don't go in to work fighting today; rather go in seeking to flow in with a light touch.

Prayer

Dear Father, make me gentle today with all those I have to rub shoulders with.

---

[1] *Robertson's Word Pictures,* e-sword.net
[2] Biblehub.com on *chrēstotēs*

DAY THIRTY-SEVEN

Rejoice

Phil.3:1

Finally, my brothers, rejoice in the Lord. To write the same things to you is no trouble to me and is safe for you.

We now come to a natural turning point in the letter, where Paul dropped in the word "finally". This is always a source of amusement for most preachers, and a source of dismay for some congregations. The word literally meant 'as for the rest', and was used in many of Paul's letters, and twice in this letter! It also meant 'furthermore' or 'in addition'.

Both the verb and the noun "rejoice" is mentioned 16 times in this letter. For Paul, therefore, it was an important theme in the life of a believer. David wrote, "You make known to me the path of life; in your presence there is fullness of joy; at your right hand are pleasures forevermore." (Psa.16:11) Pierre Teilhard de Chardin wrote:

Joy is the most infallible sign of the presence of God.[1]

C.S. Lewis wrote:

Joy is the serious business of heaven.[2]

It is important to remember at this point that this word was spoken to believers who were suffering for Christ. Roman persecution was cruel, constant and fierce, and it would have been so easy to succumb to fearful despair. There are a number of things to think about here.

Firstly, Paul was teaching the believers that their circumstances should not dictate the state of their hearts and their minds. Likewise, when we allow ourselves to be robbed of joy, the enemy wins a significant victory. The result is a listless, powerless and fatigued faith. Paul went on to say in 4:11, "I have learned in whatever situation I am in to be content." A more literal translation of this would read, 'I have learnt to

---

[1] http://www.goodreads.com/author/show/5387.Pierre_Teilhard_de _Chardin
[2] C.S. Lewis, *Letters to Malcolm: Chiefly on Prayer*, (Harvest, San Diego, 1964), pp.92-93.

be independent of any outward circumstances.' In other words, he would not allow outward events to affect what was going on inside him.

Secondly, the source of this rejoicing was to be found 'in the Lord', or more accurately 'in the sphere of the Lord'. It did not come from some stoical resilience to life, or even by favourable circumstances. Incidentally, the word 'happy' is derived from the Latin word *hap*, which has to do with what 'happens' to us. Paul was writing about something totally different. Our joy is not to be found in what happens to us; it is to be found in our relationship with Christ. He is the rock and therefore the joy of our lives – everything else is secondary and, to be honest, flawed.

Thirdly, it is significant that this word was being spoken by an imprisoned man, languishing in a Roman jail. It probably would have more sense to us if it were a word spoken by free believers to Paul.

It was such an important word that Paul was happy repeating it, knowing how beneficial it was for them to get hold of this word "rejoice". Nehemiah had written centuries earlier that "the joy of the LORD is your strength". (Neh.8:10) To "rejoice in the Lord" was a safeguard to their faith, and it is to ours. The joy of the Lord is our strength against the enemy's tactics. We need to see the Lord for who he really is, and let that vision fill and enlarge our hearts.

Thought

Joy is the atmosphere of heaven. It is an unspeakable torrent.

Prayer

Lord, let me capture today in my spirit something of the atmosphere around you.

DAY THIRTY-EIGHT

Watch Out for the Dogs (1)

Phil.3:2

Look out for the dogs, look out for the evildoers, look out for those who mutilate the flesh.

Not only is the word "rejoice" mentioned 16 times in Paul's letter to the Philippians, it is mentioned 72 times in the whole of the New Testament. The corresponding word "joy" – *chara* – is found 60 times. I love this quote from Robert Schuller:

Joy is not the absence of suffering. It is the presence of God.[1]

I believe that joy is not the filling of our hearts with the joy of knowing Christ, it is also a chosen attitude or viewpoint. William Blake wrote:

Where others see but the dawn coming over the hill, I see the soul of God shouting for joy.[2]

There was a certain group of people in the church at Jerusalem who were very unhappy with Paul's ministry. Wherever Paul went, they followed him, seeking to undermine his work. They were called the Judaizers, otherwise known as the circumcision party. These were Jews who had become Christians, but they were insisting that the Law of Moses should be adhered to and that all Gentile converts should submit to the rite of circumcision. They felt that Paul had betrayed his spiritual heritage in that he was not bringing people into "the fold of Abraham's bosom"[3]. Instead, however, he was bringing them into a 'new fold' – the church of Jesus Christ in which "there is neither Jew nor Greek, there is neither slave nor free, there is no male and female, for you are all one in Christ Jesus". (Gal.3:28)

There are people in and around the church that we need to avoid like the plague. They are locked into religion, and they cannot cope with any

---

1   http://www.joy4u.org/Quotes/JoyQuotes.htm
2   http://www.azquotes.com/quote/815441
3   Luke 16:22 (J.B. Phillips)

kind of freedom in Christ. Paul hated what these people were doing, and he reserved some of his strongest language for them. His opening word is instructive. He said, "Beware..." (NASB), "look out..." (ESV/KJV). The word *blepō* meant 'to see', and intimated that the believers should 'be constantly observing with a view to avoiding'. This was all about spiritual discernment. Paul was saying to them, and also to us, "Keep your eyes open."

On one hand, as Christians, we should be the most gentle and tolerant group of all people, but on the other hand, we should not be the most naïve or stupid. A very helpful scripture that came to me when I was put in a position of trying to judge what was true and what was false is found in Jn.2:23-25: "Now when he was in Jerusalem at the Passover Feast, many believed in his name when they saw the signs that he was doing. But Jesus on his part did not entrust himself to them, because he knew all people and needed no one to bear witness about man, for he himself knew what was in man."

Jesus himself warned of "false prophets who would come in sheep's clothing". (Matt.7:15) Paul, praying with the elders of the church at Ephesus on the beach at Miletus, told them, "I know that after my departure fierce wolves will come in among you, not sparing the flock..." (Acts 20:29) The attacks against us will come from both outside and inside the church. Keep your eyes open. Be wise and beware.

Thought

Spiritual discernment and wisdom are the eyes of the church.

Prayer

Lord, clear my senses so that I may see what is really going on today.

DAY THIRTY-NINE

Watch Out for the Dogs (2)

Phil.3:2

Look out for the dogs, look out for the evildoers, look out for those who mutilate the flesh.

Kenneth Wuest says that the Judaizers were "nominal Christians, who had accepted the Lord Jesus as the Saviour of Israel only, and who taught that a Gentile had to come through the gate of Judaism in order to be saved"[1]. In his letter to the Galatians, Paul called them "false brothers" (Gal.2:4)

This issue could have split the early church. In Acts 15:1-29, we can read of the council being held at Jerusalem to debate it. In fact, David Bosch, looking at the life of the church in Jerusalem, noted that there were three groupings: there was a 'centre wing' represented by James the half-brother of Jesus; a 'left wing' represented by Peter and John; and a 'right wing' represented by the circumcision party who were unwilling to concede a mission to Gentiles without them observing Mosaic law.[2]

Notice that there was a threefold repetition of the word "beware"[3] or "look out". That fact is important. We must never underestimate the twisted and subtle strategies of Satan.

Paul used very strong language to describe these Judaizers. The first word he chose was "dogs". The Greek word was *kunas*, and this is exactly the same term that the Jews used to describe the Gentiles. It was also used to describe those who were impudent and shameless. One commentator said that the word described "a mangy, flea-bitten, vicious and starved scavenger"[4]. The circumcision party, then, were like dogs, who were nastily snapping at his heels to draw blood, whereas they

---

1   Kenneth Wuest, *Word Studies in the Greek New Testament,* Vol.2, (Eerdmans, Michigan, 1973), p.87
2   David J. Bosch, *Transforming Mission,* (Orbis Books, New York, 2008), p.45
3   e.g. GNB
4   Kenneth Wuest, *Word Studies in the Greek New Testament,* Vol.2, (Eerdmans, Michigan, 1973), p.87

should have been sat at the table enjoying the extravagant blessing of God.

He then called them "evildoers" – better translated 'evil advocates of the necessity of works'. These people were 'workers', and they were in the church, but the modifier is that they were *evil* workers. In his letter to the believers in Corinth, he called them "deceitful workmen". (2.Cor.11:13) They were destructive rather than constructive. They were an intransigent 'old school', clinging on to the ancient faith of Israel, and deliberately sowing dissent. When people feel that they have to fight for the old models, they can be often working against the Spirit of God. Solomon wrote, "Say not, 'Why were the former days better than these?' For it is not from wisdom that you ask this." (Eccles.7:10)

Paul then goes on to call them the "mutilat[ors]". In the Greek language, this is a play on words, and is only found here. This is not 'circumcision', which actually means 'to cut around' – this is 'concision', which is 'to cut to pieces'. To a zealous Judaizer, there was little difference between the collecting of Gentile foreskins to the Red Indian collecting the scalps of the white men; it was all outward show.

For those who wished to mingle the old with the new, Jesus taught that new wine needed new wineskins. The old order of Judaism would never hold the new work of the kingdom of heaven. What God had done through the death of Christ was not an addition to the old order of Judaism – it was a new thing altogether. To insist that "this is how we have always done it" is to resist the Holy Spirit. This attitude is damaging to the work of God and must be fiercely guarded against.

Thought

Someone has rightly said, "A rut is a grave with the ends knocked out."

Prayer

Father, keep me ever open to fresh movements of the Holy Spirit.

DAY FORTY

We are the Circumcision

Phil.3:3

For we are the circumcision, who worship by the Spirit of God and glory in Christ Jesus and put no confidence in the flesh...

These Judaizers, who were troubling the church, had accepted Christ, but for them, Christ had become merely a 'bolt-on' to their Jewish faith. They had recognised that Jesus was the Messiah, but felt that the old ways of Judaism were also important. Their faith in Christ needed to be supplemented by the law. The underlying message that they were putting forward here was that Christ, and the work of the cross, were not sufficient for our salvation. Paul felt that they were "mutilating the message of the gospel by adding law to grace..."[1]

Paul answered these people by saying to the church that "we are the circumcision". The word "true" (NASB) is not in the Greek text. Paul was not saying here that there was a true and a false circumcision; he was merely saying there was only one. What did he mean by this? We must return to the book Genesis to understand this rite of circumcision, realizing that the Jews placed a lot of faith in it. There were various elements of this rite.

Firstly, it was a sign of the covenant made between Abraham and God in Gen.17:1-11. It was later embodied in the Law of Moses. It was something initiated by God, and Abraham responded with an act of obedience. From Gen.15:6, we can see that the relationship with God was already there. Circumcision, therefore, did not bring about the relationship; it merely confirmed it. Later, however, it would be used to establish the relationship. We can see the switch taking place in Jewish thinking. In the time of Christ, Jews related circumcision to Moses, not Abraham. Jesus, Stephen and Paul corrected this. (Jn.7:22 / Acts 7:8 / Rom.4:10,11)

Secondly, this rite originated out of an act of obedient faith; later it became a mode of entrance to the faith. What started as an act of faith

---

[1] Kenneth Wuest, *Word Studies in the Greek New Testament,* Vol.2, (Eerdmans, Michigan, 1973), p.87

slowly became a means of faith. Instead of resulting from the favour of God, it began to become a means of obtaining the favour of God.

God's heart is always set on 'inner reality', not outward forms that become clinical realities devoid of spiritual life. And so, in Deut.10:16, God commanded the people to circumcise the foreskin of their hearts. (cf. Deut.30:6 / Jer.4:4 / Jer.9:25,26) The real circumcision, then, in God's eyes, was an inner matter rather than an outer matter.

There is nothing new under the sun. God does a work in the earth and we latch on to it; and because it is visible and tangible, we start to relate to what God has done, rather than to the God who did it. We can then find ourselves having more of a relationship with the experiences and outward signs of God than with God himself. When God moves on, doing another new thing, we have problems, because it is not like the old thing. The kingdom of heaven, in both Christ's and Paul's eyes, was not the same as that of Jewish thinking. And so, when the 'outer' and the 'visible' take precedence, then we have missed our way. We have to learn that we walk with God and not his methods.

Thought

A manifestation of God quickly becomes a memory that we can indeed cherish, but we must not serve or worship. Only the living God himself is to be worshipped and followed.

Prayer

Dear Lord, help me not to get caught up in where you have been, but in where you are going.

DAY FORTY-ONE

The Real Circumcision

Phil.3:3

For we are the circumcision, who worship by the Spirit of God and glory in Christ Jesus and put no confidence in the flesh...

Paul was right to be angry. The circumcision party was decimating the church, attacking the new believers on three fronts. Firstly, they had turned what was originally a confirming sign of one's faith in God into a mode of entrance into the faith. Circumcision was never intended to be a doorway, but a picture on a wall.

Secondly, they were insisting that the new Gentile believers adhered to certain aspects of the law. They insisted that faith in Christ needed to be supplemented by submitting to circumcision, Sabbath-keeping and certain food laws. They were actually saying that the cross was insufficient. Paul was firm: it's not what we do to get saved, but what Christ has completely and powerfully done on the cross.

Thirdly, they wanted the 'new wine' to be kept in 'old wineskins'. Paul was angered by this imposition of the old system on to the completed act of Christ on the cross. This group of people, these "dogs", these "workers of evil", were cutting the flock to pieces. So Paul wrote and spoke clearly and strongly. Salvation is always by grace and faith, never by works. Good works are the result of an authentic salvation, not the road to it. (Eph.2:8-10)

Paul now responded by saying, "We are the real circumcision..." The NASB has "the true circumcision". However, the NIV has it correctly in saying "for it is we who are the circumcision". The emphasis is on the 'we'. What was he saying here?

Firstly, he was saying that our circumcision is a spiritual one. It is not made by human hands but by Christ. It is a circumcision of the heart. Paul writes elsewhere, "For no one is a Jew who is merely one outwardly, nor is circumcision outward and physical. But a Jew is one inwardly, and circumcision is a matter of the heart, by the Spirit, not by the letter." (Rom.2:28,29) He writes again to the Colossians, "In him also you were circumcised with a circumcision made without hands, by putting off the body of the flesh, by the circumcision of Christ..." (Col.2:11) This means that the power of our sinful nature was broken by the death of Christ on the cross, and that we do not have to sin any more. Our sinful nature is not thereby eradicated, but it has lost its dominating place in our lives. It now has no more power than we allow it to have.

Secondly, Paul is simply referring them back to the scriptures, which they should have known. Moses says in Deut.10:16, "Circumcise therefore the foreskin of your heart, and be no longer stubborn…" In Deut.30:6, he writes, "And the LORD your God will circumcise your heart and the heart of your offspring, so that you will love the LORD your God with all your heart and with all your soul, that you may live." Speaking of Abraham to the believers in Rome, Paul says, "He received the sign of circumcision as a seal of the righteousness that he had by faith while he was still uncircumcised." (Rom.4:11) So, circumcision, in the Old Testament was a seal, a sign of an already existing faith-filled relationship with God; it did not produce it. We, who know that the power of sin has been broken by the work of the cross, are the circumcision. As we walk on with God, therefore, sin should begin to become a rarity.

Thought

Jesus has done it all. All you need to do is believe.

Prayer

Father, help me to see just how great was your Son's work on the cross.

DAY FORTY-TWO

Signs of Authenticity

Phil.3:3

*For we are the circumcision, who worship by the Spirit of God
and glory in Christ Jesus and put no confidence in the flesh...*

Bishop Lightfoot made three wonderful observations on Paul's
comments:

*Firstly, it is not external but internal, not made with hands
but by the Spirit; secondly, it divests not only a part of the
flesh, but the whole body of carnal affections; thirdly, it is the
circumcision not of Moses or the Patriarchs, but of Christ.[1]*

Thus we see its uniqueness in its internal character, its full extent and
its author being Christ.

Paul now outlines three signs of authenticity, or, if you like, three
community markers for true believers. The first is that the authentic
saints are the ones "who worship by the Spirit of God". The word
translated "worship" is the Greek word *latreuō*, and it actually meant
'public worship', i.e. worship that is performed within the community of
believers. Another word for 'worship' is *proskuneō*, which meant 'to kiss
the hand', speaking of a more intimate form of worship. Paul is
emphasising that new believers were not called only to a privatised and
individual worship of God, but also to a corporate expression of worship.
God's big idea has always been the church – the corporate body of Christ,
and it is among ordinary 'flesh and blood' saints of God that we are called
to worship him – together.

Secondly, authentic worship is rooted in the inspiration and power of
the Holy Spirit. This needs to speak deeply to us. Many attend churches
whose quality of worship is far more determined by tempo, volume,
passion and style of the songs. Others are more attracted by mere
aesthetics – the atmosphere, the gothic decorations and beautifully
crafted windows that let in streams of coloured light. This, I will suggest

---

[1] Kenneth Wuest, *Word Studies in the Greek New Testament,* Vol.2,
(Eerdmans, Michigan, 1973), p.204,205

to you, is all soulish worship, and that is recognised by the oft heard statement, "The worship didn't do anything for me today." Let's be clear here: worship by the Holy Spirit is not primarily designed to do anything for us at all; it is designed to exalt and lift up the Lord. Our pleasure is simply the pleasure of having pleased him.

Thirdly, it underlines that all our activity should be in the Spirit of God. Jesus told the Samaritan woman that "the hour is coming, and is now here, when the true worshipers will worship the Father in spirit and truth, for the Father is seeking such people to worship him. God is spirit, and those who worship him must worship in spirit and truth." (Jn.4:23) Paul wrote that he served the Lord in the realms of his spirit. (Rom.1:9) Accordingly, our worship, our service, our ministry must never be guided by what we see, hear and feel; it must be inspired and directed by the Holy Spirit, who whispers and speaks and is present and active in our spirits – that deepest part of our being. We must learn to become intimate with the Holy Spirit, discerning his movements, his direction and his voice, and worship under his leadership.

Thought

A.W. Tozer wrote:

...song can never bring the Holy Spirit, but the Holy Spirit does invariably bring song.[1]

There is sometimes a difference between what we are looking for in worship and what the Lord is looking for. They really ought to be the same.

Prayer

Dear Lord, please make our worship more about you and less about us.

---

[1]   A.W. Tozer, *The Divine Conquest,* (Oliphants, London, 1965), p.73

DAY FORTY-THREE

Signs of Authenticity (2)

Phil.3:3

For we are the circumcision, who worship by the Spirit of God and glory in Christ Jesus and put no confidence in the flesh...

We need not worry about making much of the Holy Spirit, because he loves to make much of the Lord Jesus. A.W. Tozer wrote that the first sign of the baptism in the Spirit is...

...a heightened sense of the presence of Christ. He is felt to be a real Person and to be intimately, ravishingly near.[1]

Jesus, speaking of the Holy Spirit said, "He will teach you all things and bring to your remembrance all that I have said to you;" (Jn.14:26) "He will bear witness about me;" (Jn.15:26) "He will glorify me." (Jn.16:4)

The second authentic sign or 'community marker' of true spirituality is that they "glory in Christ Jesus". This is one of Paul's favourite words. It is *kauchaomai*, and it is found 35 times in his writings. It literally means 'to take pride in, to exult in, to boast about', and it has a strong sense of exuberance and excitement. Many commentators feel that one of Paul's favourite OT passages was Jer.9:23,24: "Let not the wise man boast in his wisdom, let not the mighty man boast in his might, let not the rich man boast in his riches, but let him who boasts boast in this, that he understands and knows me, that I am the LORD who practices steadfast love, justice, and righteousness in the earth. For in these things I delight, declares the LORD."

Stuart Briscoe wrote:

There are some things that are so meaningful to us that we have to speak with enthusiasm about them.[2]

This is more than being inwardly thrilled and excited; this is being vocal about it. The apostle Peter said to a hostile Sanhedrin who sought

---

[1]   A.W. Tozer, *The Divine Conquest,* (Oliphants, London, 1965), p.91
[2]   Stuart Briscoe, *Bound for Joy,* (Regal Books, California, 1982), 104

to prevent the disciples from speaking about Jesus, "We cannot but speak of what we have seen and heard." (Acts 4:20)

Sometimes, we can, in our ignorance, equate demonstrative, exuberant behaviour and language with extremism or emotionalism. Was David any less a king when he danced with all his might before the ark of God? There were those who thought he demeaned himself. (2.Sam.6:20) I have heard that Lincoln football supporters do not get overexcited when their side scores a goal. Maybe that is a cultural thing. The circumcision party rooted for Moses; Paul, on the other hand, rooted for Jesus Christ. For him, Moses slipped into the background when compared with what Jesus had accomplished.

Here was joy unspeakable! Here was the presence! God with us – Emmanuel! Paul would remember that "in your presence there is fullness of joy". (Psa.16:11) Briscoe comments that for Paul…

> …there was no preacher in his cell, no beautiful church building in the prison, no hymn book to sing from and no fellowship to enjoy…[1]

Here is a challenge: What or who excites us? Are we able to boast about Jesus Christ in such a way that our neighbours and friends get a little jealous? Paul was so excited about Christ that he spoke of him often, enthusiastically. The church that is boasting about the Lord Jesus is demonstrating a true and authentic sign of spirituality.

Thought

What fills your heart will come out of your mouth. What are you talking much about?

Prayer

Father, let the glorious reality of Your Son move and excite me today.

---

[1] Ibid, p.105

DAY FORTY-FOUR

Signs of Authenticity (3)

Phil.3:3

For we are the circumcision, who worship by the Spirit of God and glory in Christ Jesus and put no confidence in the flesh...

We are continuing to look at Paul's three marks of authentic spirituality, or authentic church. The first was a corporate experience of worship inspired, energised and led by the Holy Spirit. The second was being so in love with and so excited about the Lord Jesus that we boasted about him. Any authentic church will major both on the Holy Spirit and on the Lord Jesus. We would expect that Paul would go on to mention the Father. He doesn't, but instead, he makes this surprising turn by saying that the people who make up authentic church do not major on themselves. They "put no confidence in the flesh".

Firstly, what does he mean by "the flesh"? Alec Motyer wrote that the term denotes "man at his highest pinnacle of development and at his lowest point of failure"[1]. Calvin writes of Paul as teaching that "he gives the name of flesh to everything that is apart from Christ"[2]. It is, in fact, all that is 'natural' and 'human'. It is both our physical body, and also our inner natural feelings and emotions. This is the point: our new birth is by the Spirit of God, and in order to progress and become fruitful in the spiritual life, it will always be by the Spirit and never by our own energies and inclinations. Good as natural humanity may be, it is actually, according to the Scriptures, "hostile to God" (Rom.8:7) and "fights against the Spirit" (Gal.5:17). Our intelligence, our zeal, our good ideas and our natural strengths can all combine to actually counteract the workings and purposes of God. Many a work of the kingdom has foundered because men have sought to help God out. Solomon would

---

[1]   Alec Motyer, *The Message of Philippians,* BST series, (IVP, Leicester, 1984), p.152

[2]   John Calvin, *Calvin's Commentary on the Bible* – Commentary on Philippians 3:3, www.studylight.org/commentaries/cal/philippians-3.html, 1840-57.

write, "Trust in the LORD with all your heart, and do not lean on your own understanding." (Prov.3:5) Jesus would put it more bluntly: "I am the vine; you are the branches. Whoever abides in me and I in him, he it is that bears much fruit, for apart from me you can do nothing." (Jn.15:5) All our inspiration and strength must come out of our relationship with Christ. We need to be open and receptive to letting heaven speak vision, direction and strength into our lives.

Paul went on to say that authentic spirituality "places no confidence" in the flesh, in our natural humanity or abilities. The same word translated "confidence" is used is Phil.1:25 where it is translated "convinced". In fact, he wrote to the believers in Rome, "For I know that nothing good dwells in me, that is, in my flesh." (Rom.7:18) The balance, therefore, is not to have confidence in ourselves, but to have absolute confidence in Christ in us.

Jesus began the Sermon on the Mount with these words: "Blessed are the poor in spirit, for theirs is the kingdom of heaven." The word "poor" there is *ptōchos*, which means 'utterly destitute'. There is another word for 'poor', and that is *penēs*, describing a man who has to work for his living. The Greeks also defined such a man as *autodiakonos*, meaning 'to help and serve myself'. Such a person, although poor, had confidence in himself, feeling that he could muddle through and make something of his life and ministry. The word that Jesus chose to use, *ptōchos*, described one who has no confidence in himself. He is in the right place to receive all the help he needs from heaven.

Thought

Stop trying to give God a hand, because it usually ends in tears!

Prayer

Lord, please reveal to my heart how deceptive self-confidence can be.

DAY FORTY-FIVE

Paul's Pedigree

Phil.3:4-6

...though I myself have reason for confidence in the flesh also. If anyone else thinks he has reason for confidence in the flesh, I have more: circumcised on the eighth day, of the people of Israel, of the tribe of Benjamin, a Hebrew of Hebrews; as to the law, a Pharisee; as to zeal, a persecutor of the church; as to righteousness under the law, blameless.

Having outlined the three authentic community markers or 'signs' of authentic church, Paul now began to enlarge on the third – having "no confidence in the flesh". Let me quote Alec Motyer again, but in full:

Flesh sums up what a person is apart from the grace of Christ – the human being as yet unchanged by God's regenerating and redeeming work. It covers man at his highest pinnacle of development and at his lowest point of failure.

Paul taught here that even the best we can become in and of ourselves doesn't come close to scratching it with God, and we are foolish to think that is does.

He then proved the point by outlining his own religious pedigree. His religious upbringing, experience and training, and his pedigree were the finest. It's interesting that he outlined seven aspects. That is a good number for a Jew – it spoke of perfection! They were broken down into four aspects of national heritage and three aspects of religious achievements.

Real Jews were circumcised on the eighth day of their life. Ishmaelites, on the other hand, were initiated by this rite when they were thirteen years old (as Ishmael was), and Gentile converts (proselytes) were initiated when they were fully grown men. Paul, therefore, was a real Jew. He was born an Israelite and came from the tribe of Benjamin. Benjamin was called "the beloved of the Lord" in Deut.33:12. They were the most loyal of the tribes. He was also "a Hebrew of Hebrews" – in other words, both his parents were Jewish; he was not a racial mongrel.

Bishop Lightfoot noted that a man may be a Jew because he could trace his ancestry back to Jacob, but he was not a Hebrew unless he could speak the ancient language. Paul was not some Hellenized Jew who would be reading the Scriptures in the Greek translation. He was a thoroughbred of the old school!

Paul had also been a Pharisee, the strictest of all the Jewish sects. (Acts 26:5) He had studied under Gamaliel, who was one of the greatest of rabbis of his time. Paul most probably would have known the Hebrew Scriptures by heart.

Paul was so zealous for God that he angrily persecuted the church (Acts 26:9-11), considering it a duty to God in preserving the purity of the Jewish faith. When it came to zeal for the honour of God, in his view, he was far ahead of anyone else. He closed this list by commenting on his personal religious integrity; as far as he was concerned, he was faultless.

From a religious point of view, the list was very impressive; for religious pedigree and achievement, there were not many who could touch him. But Paul's background and works were, unfortunately, designed to impress the Almighty, to create an aura of excellence and perfection.

God's verdict, on the other hand, was totally different. In God's eyes, Paul's outward righteousness was nothing but a bunch of dirty rags. (Isa.64:6) And that's how Paul eventually came to see it as well.

Thought

God is never fooled by our pretensions of holy behaviour.

Prayer

Dear Lord, let my outer life be a true reflection of what is happening within me.

DAY FORTY-SIX

The Power of Passions

Phil.3:7

But whatever gain I had, I counted as loss for the sake of Christ.

I find it intriguing that Paul was majoring so much on having no confidence in natural qualifications and abilities. In writing about authentic church, one would think that he would have majored on corporate worship in the Spirit rather than stressing his religious background. The truth is that natural spirituality is an oxymoron. Much was made, throughout his writings, about the conflict between 'soulish' and 'natural' activity, and that which was inspired and empowered by the Holy Spirit – "the unforced rhythms of grace", as Peterson calls the way of Christ in Matt.11:29. Paul had come to the personal conclusion that, "I know that good does not live in me – that is, in my human nature." (Rom.7:18, GNB)

And so Paul really turned the heat on his pedigree and achievements, and wrote, "Whatever gain I had, I count as loss…" The New English Bible (NEB) puts it, "…all such assets I have written off…" In the business world, this would seem an absolutely topsy-turvy thing to do. In The Message it reads, "The very credentials these people are waving around as something special, I'm tearing up and throwing out with the trash – along with everything else I used to take credit for." God was not impressed by his efforts. Alec Motyer wrote:

> *We learn that Christ does not become ours by effort, but by the rejection of effort.*

In the Greek text, the word "gain" is actually in the plural and the word "loss" is in the singular. Ralph Martin writes:

> *Because of all that Christ had become to him, Paul is willing to collect all his former privileges … to put them, as it were, in one parcel, and write that off as loss. He is not content simply to dismiss them, and become indifferent to them.*

Rather ... he rejects them with horror, and treats them as liabilities.

The phrase "I counted" is in the perfect tense, speaking of an action in the past that is effective in the future. In other words, Paul's decision was not a gradual persuasion that crept up on him; it was rather a dramatic and sudden life-changing decision, resulting in a face-to-face encounter with the risen Jesus on the Damascus road. On one hand, he had all his pedigree and achievements, and they sparkled in his eyes. God then placed Jesus Christ before him on the other hand, and as Paul then made the comparison, that which sparkled suddenly wilted, and Paul then blew it all away.

The reason this valuation was taken was "for the sake of Christ". Paul, in the light of Jesus Christ, suddenly weighed up everything he was, and had become, and saw that it was utterly worthless. In the face of Jesus, all his human achievements paled into insignificance.

We must not seek to impress God, or to impress others. Rather, we need to be impressed with God and with Jesus Christ. And actually, if the truth be known, without you and I having to do anything, he is impressed with us already.

Thought

To see our heart and motives and our perceived spirituality as God sees them would be quite a shock to many of us. How open are we to hearing his verdicts?

Prayer

Lord, give me a true sense of how I stand before you, and help me to live accordingly.

DAY FORTY-SEVEN

Paul's Valuation

Phil.4:8 (NLT)

Finally, brothers, whatever is true, whatever is honorable, whatever is just, whatever is pure, whatever is lovely, whatever is commendable, if there is any excellence, if there is anything worthy of praise, think about these things.

John Paton was a missionary translator who one day was struggling to find a word for 'faith' in the local dialect. He was interrupted in his studies by a man needing help. The man said to him, "Please, can I come and lean heavily on you?" Suddenly, there for him was his translation. Faith is 'leaning heavily' upon Christ.[1] Paul no longer leaned on his pedigree or his achievements; he leaned heavily on Christ. Paul threw his impressive religious crutches away and fell into the arms of Jesus. The word 'loss' is an old word in the Greek language. It is *zēmian*, and carries with it, not just a sense of loss, but of damage. Paul's pedigree and religious achievements were actually damaging to his walk with God.

Our human efforts to achieve heavenly recognition and acceptance are self-defeating and destructive. Even the 'helping of God along' can be counterproductive. Biblical effort comes out of a vital relationship with Christ. It is different because it is inspired and empowered.

Philippians 3:8-11 is one long sentence in the original Greek language. (cp. Eph.1:3-14) Permit me to make a little aside here. Gordon Fee says that this is one of the truly "surpassing moments in the Pauline corpus; it would be a tragedy if its splendour were lost in analysis"[2]. On the dangers of overcritical studies of the Bible, Eugene Peterson shows his perception when he writes:

We obscure the form when we atomize Scripture by dissecting it, analysing it like a specimen in the laboratory. Every detail of Scripture is worth pursuing endlessly; no scholarly attention expended over this text is ever wasted. But when the

---

[1]   Cited by Alec Motyer, *The Message of Philippians,* BST series, (IVP, Leicester, 1984), p.159

[2]   Gordon Fee, *Paul's Letter to the Philippians,* (Eerdmans, Michigan, 1995)

impersonal objective of the laboratory technician replaces the adoring dalliance of a lover, we end up with file drawers full of information, organised for our convenience as occasions present themselves. It ceases to function as revelation for us.[1]

Like Ezra in the Old Testament, we must set ourselves, not only to study the Scriptures, but to practise them, and then to teach them. (Ezra.7:1) The order is significant.

Chrysostom once said that "when the sun appears, it is a loss to sit by a candle"[2]. Paul wrote, in the light of his blinding experience on the Damascus road, "Indeed, I count everything as loss because of the surpassing worth of knowing Christ Jesus my Lord." Knowing Jesus was of infinitely more worth than anything else this world could offer. The Greek word he used was *huperechon*, and it meant 'to hold above as far superior'.

Of all the things that people pursue, many of them quite admirable, there is absolutely nothing that compares with the personal knowledge of Jesus Christ. This, to me, is a sharply focusing scripture. We need to stop and ask ourselves: What exactly are we pursuing? What, or who is more important to us? Here in the West, surrounded by multiple options and many desirable pursuits, we need to ensure that a personal and intimate knowledge of Jesus Christ is the main, the central and the most important focus of our lives.

Thought

To know Christ, and to become like him, is the finest single goal of a human life.

Prayer

Father, show me the futility of any pursuit that does not bring me closer to your Son.

---

[1] Eugene Peterson, *Eat this Book – the art of spiritual reading,* (Hodder & Stoughton, London, 2006), p.46

[2] Charles Ellicott, *Commentary of the Whole Bible,* Vol.8, Eph to Rev, (Wipf & Stock, Oregon,1897), p.81

DAY FORTY-EIGHT

Paul's Goals

Phil.3:8-11

Indeed, I count everything as loss because of the surpassing worth of knowing Christ Jesus my Lord. For his sake I have suffered the loss of all things and count them as rubbish, in order that I may gain Christ and be found in him, not having a righteousness of my own that comes from the law, but that which comes through faith in Christ, the righteousness from God that depends on faith – that I may know him and the power of his resurrection, and may share his sufferings, becoming like him in his death, that by any means possible I may attain the resurrection from the dead.

Paul's experience of Christ had opened his eyes to the utter worthlessness of his own credentials, achievements and abilities, and also to the surpassing worth of being in a personal and close relationship with the Lord Jesus. That relationship came to mean more to him than anything that the world could offer him. There are so many seemingly worthwhile activities and things that can creep in to distract us. We need to jealously guard our walk with him from anything that would lead us away from this.

I think of the little scenario in Luke's Gospel (Lk.10:38-42) where Jesus came to the house of Mary and Martha in Bethany. Jesus sat there, teaching, and Mary sat there, listening to him. That was the agenda for that moment. Martha, however, found herself "distracted by much serving" and ended up being "anxious and troubled about many things". The lesson was that there was a time for serving and a time for sitting at the feet of Jesus. There was also a clear message about which order the serving and the sitting came. We have to learn of the negative power of distraction for our own spiritual good.

Paul wrote that he has actually suffered the loss of "all things" for the sake of Christ. We are not told what they are, but we are left with the distinct impression that it included a lot more than just his religious pedigree and religious achievements. It could have included the love of his family, his independence and his personal ambitions. It did include,

112

at times, the skin off his back and his freedom, and it would soon include the loss of his life. But were they seen as loss by a man so in love with Christ? Look at the passion recorded in Acts 20:24: "I do not account my life of any value nor as precious to myself, if only I may finish my course and the ministry that I received from the Lord Jesus, to testify to the gospel of the grace of God." And also in Acts 21:13: "What are you doing, weeping and breaking my heart? For I am ready not only to be imprisoned but even to die in Jerusalem for the name of the Lord Jesus."

He then used another word to describe what he felt about his losses. He had counted them as "rubbish" (ESV/NIV), "garbage" (NLT). The word in Greek is *skubala*, which meant "either excrement or what is thrown away from the table"[1]. It is translated in the KJV as "dung", but can also more graphically mean 'foul smelling street garbage' fit only for dogs. It is as if Paul had picked a word that would describe that which to him was the most revolting, the worst ever. Why such fierce language?

The answer is found in two words: 'comparison' and 'passion'. One view of Jesus Christ, and Paul's value systems were thrown in utter disarray. Paul passionately loved God as he saw him, and he loved the Scriptures as he understood them, and those perceptions had driven him into a fierce jealousy for God's name and honour. But once he saw the face of Christ, he fell in love with him, and he also fell in love with all the saints who made up his body. I don't think the zeal really ever left him. Instead, it became sharply focused in the right place, and the anger was replaced by love.

Thought

Focus is eroded by the powerful onslaughts of distraction.

Prayer

Lord, help me to separate what you have called me to from the bleating of distractions.

---

[1] *Vincent's Word Studies,* e-sword.net

DAY FORTY-NINE

The Greater Grace

Phil.3:8-11

Indeed, I count everything as loss because of the surpassing worth of knowing Christ Jesus my Lord. For his sake I have suffered the loss of all things and count them as rubbish, in order that I may gain Christ and be found in him, not having a righteousness of my own that comes from the law, but that which comes through faith in Christ, the righteousness from God that depends on faith – that I may know him and the power of his resurrection, and may share his sufferings, becoming like him in his death, that by any means possible I may attain the resurrection from the dead.

In Acts 27:13-24, Paul wrote of the time when he, among others, was shipwrecked at sea. In the story, at certain dangerous moments, they began to jettison firstly the cargo, then the equipment and then the wheat. (27:18,19,38) That which was precious to them had become a dangerous liability. In the same way, Paul jettisoned what was previously precious to him in order to gain Christ. All that he had accrued up to that point was now threatening to wreck his walk with God.

There is a change in the tenses regarding the loss of all things. In verse 7 he says, "But whatever gain I had, I counted as loss for the sake of Christ." And in verse 8, he says, "Indeed, I count everything as loss..." The word "counted" is in the past tense and the word "count" is in the present tense. In other words, years later, he was still counting them as refuse.

Here, then, we have an exchange. Paul had exchanged his impressive past for a future walk with Christ. More than that, he had reckoned that all he had suffered was for the sake of Jesus Christ. His view on suffering was wonderful. Whether it was because of his own actions, or the actions of others, or even circumstantial, he did not gripe about what had happened to him; he saw it in fact as a gain. It was all in order to gain Christ.

What does it mean "to gain Christ"? The word is *kerdēsō*, and Vine's Dictionary of New Testament words says that it describes "the means of so practically appropriating Christ to oneself that he becomes the dominating power in and over one's whole being and circumstances"[1]. This was not describing his conversion experience; this was describing his lifetime experience of the surrendering of all things to Christ that he might gain all of him. Homer Kent, in the NIV Bible Commentary, wrote:

> *Although at regeneration a person receives Christ, this is only the beginning of one's discovery of what riches this entails. In Christ all the treasures of wisdom and knowledge are hidden (Col.2:3), but to search them out and appropriate them requires a lifetime.*[2]

Christ is our treasure, and it is worth losing everything in order to obtain him. He, and his kingdom, is the pearl of greatest price; He, and his kingdom, is the field full of buried treasure. Paul was never satisfied by his present experience of Christ, but always yearned for more. He longed that his life be swamped, inundated, saturated and overflowing with the presence and the intimate friendship of Jesus. Nothing that this world could throw at him, or even offer him, came anywhere close to this gaining of Christ. Just one encounter with the risen Christ had changed everything.

In the parable of the sower, Jesus spoke of the seed that fell on thorny ground. (You can find the whole parable in Matt.13:1-23 / Mk.4:1-20 / Lk.8:4-15 – they are essential reading.) In the parable, the thorns overpowered, choked and strangled the word of the kingdom. The message was clear: Christ will not fit with other personal agendas. They will, in fact, strangle all that he is seeking to do within us. Here, then, is a question: What would you and I sacrifice in order to gain Christ in all his fullness?

Thought

What is Christ to you? A passionate relationship or a weekend hobby?

---

[1] W.E. Vine, *Vine's Expository Dictionary of Biblical Words,* (Nelson, New York, 1985), p.260

[2] Homer Kent, *Philippians, The NIV Bible Commentary,* Vol 2: NT (Zondervan, London, 1994), p.805

Prayer

Dear Holy Spirit, so work in me that the Lord Jesus becomes everything to me.

DAY FIFTY

Found in Him

Phil.3:8-11

Indeed, I count everything as loss because of the surpassing worth of knowing Christ Jesus my Lord. For his sake I have suffered the loss of all things and count them as rubbish, in order that I may gain Christ and be found in him, not having a righteousness of my own that comes from the law, but that which comes through faith in Christ, the righteousness from God that depends on faith – that I may know him and the power of his resurrection, and may share his sufferings, becoming like him in his death, that by any means possible I may attain the resurrection from the dead.

Like the man in the story of the treasure that was hidden in the field, Paul got rid of everything in order to purchase it. Everything previously valuable to him was now seen as dangerous and defiling as he contemplated his new walk with Jesus. Paul's goal – the gaining, or winning, of Christ – totally absorbed him. Would we today have felt that he was imbalanced? I remember my own father being in a rage because I was giving away stuff that I felt was hindering my new walk with the Lord.

Not only was Christ Paul's treasure, he was also his home, his shelter, his hiding place and his refuge. He wanted to be "found in Christ". Not only was Christ in him; he was also in Christ. Paul used this terminology – "in Christ" – regularly in his writings. This was the locative sphere where the believers were to be found. Often, he would write to the saints who were firstly located in Christ, and then he would mention their geographical location. "In Christ" is the place where all believers live and move and have their being; this is the sphere out of which all of us serve and minister; this is the atmosphere that we breathe in on a daily basis.

There is, firstly, a present sense to this. Paul was saying that wherever he was, whether in a prison, a boat, a courtroom, a meeting, he was in Christ. He spoke, reasoned, acted and reacted out of this context. Paul also wanted it to be evidenced. He was saying to the church, in effect, wherever and however they found him, he would be found in Christ –

influenced and inspired not by his natural surroundings but by the spiritual reality of Christ.

Then there was an eschatological (future) aspect to this. This dwelling in Christ would stand him in good stead for that final Day of Judgment when he would stand before God the Father. Piercing eyes would probe and survey him, but he would have no fear, because he was found to be in Christ. He would not be found having a righteousness of his own, but having been clothed and dressed in the spotless righteousness of Christ. The imagery is powerful. In the Old Testament, there is the prophetic vision of Zechariah, who spoke of Joshua the High Priest, standing before the LORD. The text says that "Joshua was standing before the angel, clothed with filthy garments." Satan was also stood alongside him, accusing him. Zechariah then records that "the angel said to those who were standing before him, 'Remove the filthy garments from him.' And to him he said, 'Behold, I have taken your iniquity away from you, and I will clothe you with pure vestments.'" (Zech.3:1-5) The truth is, if God has so clothed us, then we are clean. Incidentally, the Chinese character for 'righteous' is actually made up of two characters. The first and upper character is 'a lamb' while the second and lower character is the character for 'me'. It quite literally means that 'I' am covered by 'the lamb'.

Wherever we find ourselves, at home, in an office, or even in difficult circumstances, we are to be found in Christ. According to the Scriptures, however, this is our primary residence. We are in Christ, in whom we now live and move and have our being. Therefore, we are perfectly safe, secure, and we are now being influenced and inspired by him. It is this relationship, this environment, that is now shaping our lives.

Thought

"In Christ" is our primary location. How much is that affecting you?

Prayer

Lord, living in you is so refreshing, so challenging, and so adventurous!

DAY FIFTY-ONE

Speaking Against Each Other

Phil.3:8-11

Indeed, I count everything as loss because of the surpassing worth of knowing Christ Jesus my Lord. For his sake I have suffered the loss of all things and count them as rubbish, in order that I may gain Christ and be found in him, not having a righteousness of my own that comes from the law, but that which comes through faith in Christ, the righteousness from God that depends on faith – that I may know him and the power of his resurrection, and may share his sufferings, becoming like him in his death, that by any means possible I may attain the resurrection from the dead.

Isaiah the prophet wrote, "We have all become like one who is unclean, and all our righteous deeds are like a polluted garment. We all fade like a leaf, and our iniquities, like the wind, take us away." (Isa.64:6) Paul, as he approached the spotless Christ, suddenly saw his own immaculate self-righteousness becoming stained and filthy. It shocked and in fact disgusted him. All his exacting efforts were seen to have become soiled and soiling. All his fastidious attention to the law, believing that it made him presentable to God, was seen to have been of no avail whatsoever.

As he turned in his heart to the Lord Jesus, he felt the filthy rags being lifted off his shoulders and taken from him, and he then received the crisp, pristine, pure linen of the righteousness of Christ himself. It was a gift from heaven, and it covered him completely, bringing a smile to the face of the Father and the Son.

Righteousness is simply 'being in the right with God'. His own righteousness came literally 'out of the law', whereas the righteousness that God gave him came literally 'out of God'. One came out of a book; the other came out of heaven. God was the source of this righteousness, not Paul. This righteousness, according to Bishop Handley C.G. Moule, was "uncaused by anything in man"[1].

It came to Paul by faith, and this became the basis of his relationship with Christ. It was a faith in what Jesus, not Paul, had accomplished. It came through faith and was on the basis of faith. Paul wrote to the Roman believers, "But now the righteousness of God has been manifested apart from the law, although the Law and the Prophets bear witness to it – the righteousness of God through faith in Jesus Christ for all who believe." (Rom.3:21,22)

The Preacher's commentary says:

> *Too many of us Christians have yet to appropriate this freedom-bringing, wing-giving truth. We keep one foot in the law domain where "doing" prevails, hoping that our doing will lead to our being righteous. We forget that we do not strive to live by the Spirit in order to be in the Spirit. It is the reverse. Because we are in the Spirit we live by the Spirit. And because we have been conferred the righteousness of God, we do deeds of righteousness. We do righteous works not to get in right relationship with God, but because He has already justified us. We are in right relationship with Him by faith.[2]*

We receive all that God gives us by faith, and we stand where we do by faith. Faith is in itself a gift. Faith is both the means and the bedrock of our walk. Personal achievement gets us very little, except the notice and admiration of men. It is by faith that we are saved; it is by faith that we progress; it is by faith that we do exploits for God; it is by faith that we endure all that the world, and sometimes the church, throws at us. Faith is a gift to us; faith is the means for us and faith is practised by us. We are not just believers by faith; we are practitioners in and by faith.

Thought

Both faith and righteousness are gifts from God. There is nothing to earn or strive for; but everything to thank him for.

---

[1] H.C.G. Moule, *The Epistle of Paul to the Philippians,* (Cambridge Press, London,1907), p.94
[2] *The Preacher's Commentary,* e-sword.net

Prayer

Lord, all that I have, and stand upon, is from you. Thank you so, so much!

Day Fifty-Two

Knowing Christ

Phil.3:8-11

Indeed, I count everything as loss because of the surpassing worth of knowing Christ Jesus my Lord. For his sake I have suffered the loss of all things and count them as rubbish, in order that I may gain Christ and be found in him, not having a righteousness of my own that comes from the law, but that which comes through faith in Christ, the righteousness from God that depends on faith – that I may know him and the power of his resurrection, and may share his sufferings, becoming like him in his death, that by any means possible I may attain the resurrection from the dead.

There was deep purpose in Paul's thinking. He had been more than happy to lay aside his own righteousness and religious achievements for the sole purpose of knowing Christ. This knowing of Christ had filled his thinking and focused his life's direction. Everything else became subservient to it. He mentioned it in v.8, and he returned to it with a passion in v.10: "...that I may know him..." You can almost feel the intensity of his desire.

This knowing of Christ is not the learning and understanding of biblical doctrines, important though this is. It is not even the grasping of spiritual, church or leadership principles, important though they are. All of these are integral to our walk, but they are only the surrounding features of who he is. All biblical and ecclesiastical studies must lead us, not to a thorough knowledge of a system of belief, but to a deeper relationship with Christ himself. Let me quote at length A.W. Tozer:

If a man have only correct doctrine to offer me, then I am sure to slip out at the first intermission to seek the company of someone who has seen for himself how lovely is the face of him who is the Rose of Sharon and the Lily of the valley. Such a man, and only such a man, can help me.[1]

---

[1]   A.W. Tozer, *The Divine Conquest,* (Oliphants, London, 1965), p.14

Several years ago, Mo, my wife, wrote a song, and it included the lines, "Study and praying mean nothing to me, if in them Jesus I do not see." In our local church membership course, we have this statement: "All that we do and teach must deepen our awareness of, and relationship with, the Lord Jesus."

This has always been the desire of God: that we might know him, his heart, his ways and his thoughts. And this has always been the desire of any authentic man or woman of God. David yearned for God; his hunger and thirst for God himself was insatiable, and it drove him to seek him out. His worship songs expressed the beauty and the deep satisfaction of that intense and passionate relationship. It has not lessened in the New Covenant. Jesus is to be known, loved, walked with, worshipped and obeyed with a full and passionate heart.

We have to make a deliberate choice about what we give our time and attention to. This deeply knowing Christ does not happen overnight; it takes time. Every relationship that is worth its salt involves hours of loving and close dialogue. It takes time that must be deliberately allocated. You do not find the time, you make the time. Again, let us hear Tozer:

> God has not bowed to our nervous haste nor embraced the methods of the machine age. The man (or woman) who would know God must give time to Him.[1]

This 'knowledge' is not ethereal, but deeply transformative. It is not purely correct information about Christ; it is an intensely personal and profoundly experiential knowledge of Christ. This was the one goal of Paul. Everything else flowed out of this. Writing of Paul, the Cistercian monk Thomas Merton wrote that he "was qualified to be an apostle by the depth of his interior life"[2]. We can learn lots from this.

Thought

Pining is the unspoken language of deep love.

Prayer

Lord, create a strong and insatiable desire in my heart to know you.

---

[1] Ibid.
[2] Thomas Merton, *On Saint Bernard,* (Cistercian Publications, Michigan, 1980), p.32

DAY FIFTY-THREE

Knowing Resurrection

Phil.3:8-11

Indeed, I count everything as loss because of the surpassing worth of knowing Christ Jesus my Lord. For his sake I have suffered the loss of all things and count them as rubbish, in order that I may gain Christ and be found in him, not having a righteousness of my own that comes from the law, but that which comes through faith in Christ, the righteousness from God that depends on faith – that I may know him and the power of his resurrection, and may share his sufferings, becoming like him in his death, that by any means possible I may attain the resurrection from the dead.

Paul's desire to know Christ was incredibly intense. The word "know" meant 'to know by personal experience'. Müller put it this way: it meant a "personal contact of life"[1]. Talking about Jesus is totally different to walking with Jesus. It begs the question, how real is he to you?

Paul now moves to another aspect of spiritual life with Christ. He desires to know "the power of his resurrection". Again, this is an 'experienced' knowledge. Kenneth Wuest wrote that Paul wanted "to experience the same power that raised Christ from the dead surging through his own being, overcoming sin in his life and producing the Christian graces"[2].

The word "power" here meant "that which overcomes resistance"[3].

We have to realise and see that when Christ was raised from the dead, we, too, were raised with him. Paul wrote, "But God, being rich in mercy, because of the great love with which he loved us, even when we were dead in our trespasses, made us alive together with Christ ... and raised

---

[1]   Jac J. Müller, *The Epistles of Paul to the Philippians and to Philemon*, (Eerdmans, Michigan, 1980), p.115

[2]   Kenneth Wuest, *Philippians, Word Studies in the Greek New Testament*, Vol.2, (Eerdmans, Michigan, 1942) , p.93

[3]   Ibid.

us up with him and seated us with him in the heavenly places in Christ Jesus...' (Eph.2:4-6) He also wrote, "...having been buried with him in baptism, in which you were also raised with him through faith in the powerful working of God, who raised him from the dead." (Col.2:12) Resurrection is not something we achieve by faith; it is something we see by faith. It is a done deed.

Paul was not just thinking about Christ's physical resurrection. Homer Kent wrote:

> *He is not thinking only of the divine power that raised Christ from the dead, but the power of the resurrected Christ now operating in the believer's life.*[1]

It is this power which is designed to be at work in us who believe. This is the "eternal life" of which the New Testament writers speak – a life that animates, resurrects, envisions and enables us to live at a far higher level. There are those who live, and then those who are *fully alive.* The evidence that we have participated in the resurrection of Christ is that we are beginning to live at a totally different level – spiritually and morally – from those who live and work around us. This is 'higher plane living' here on earth.

I do not think that we fully appreciate what God has done for and in us. There are hints in Scripture, such as, "...for he who is in you is greater than he who is in the world." (1.Jn.4:4) Whenever we encounter rebellion or anger or lust or selfishness within and around us, the Spirit of resurrection within us wants to rise up and overpower it – overcoming all resistance to the advance of the life of Christ within us. This power resides within us. We need to recognise it, tap into it and submit to it.

Thought

Life in Christ is much, much more than we think.

Prayer

Lord, open my eyes to see exactly what happened to me when I first believed.

---

[1] Homer Kent, *Philippians,* NIV Bible Commentary, Vol.2, Hodder & Stoughton, London, 1994), p.805

DAY FIFTY-FOUR

Knowing Suffering

Phil.3:8-11

*Indeed, I count everything as loss because of the surpassing
worth of knowing Christ Jesus my Lord. For his sake I have
suffered the loss of all things and count them as rubbish, in
order that I may gain Christ and be found in him, not having
a righteousness of my own that comes from the law, but that
which comes through faith in Christ, the righteousness from
God that depends on faith – that I may know him and the
power of his resurrection, and may share his sufferings,
becoming like him in his death, that by any means possible I
may attain the resurrection from the dead.*

Baker's New Testament Commentary says of Paul, "He longs for
an ever-increasing supply of the power that proceeds from the
risen and exalted Saviour."[1] We are not called to live this Christian
life by our own ingenuity or strength; instead we are called to realise and
appropriate the life that has already been placed within us. Christians are
different because of the life that is within them.

Winston Churchill once wrote:

*If you don't have any enemies in life you have never stood up
for anything.*[2]

Anyone who is seriously in love with Jesus, and is manifesting the
power of the risen Jesus in his life, will eventually experience suffering.
Paul actually called it "the fellowship of his suffering", and he expressed
a strong desire to know it by experience. But let us be clear about this:
Paul was no masochist. He simply realised that, to quote Amy
Carmichael, the missionary to India, "The nearer the soldier is to the
Captain the more he will be attacked by the enemy."[3] The early

---

[1] *Baker's New Testament Commentary,* e-sword.net
[2] http://www.azquotes.com/quote/850323
[3] Frank Houghton, *Amy Carmichael of Dohnavur,* (SPCL, London, 1953),
     p.219

Christians were not thrown to the lions because they were rebellious citizens – they simply exposed the corruptness and falsities of the state by their pure devotion and love for Christ.

In the Gospel accounts, the sufferings of Christ came before his resurrection. Many desire the power of Christ but shrink from the sufferings of Christ. But they go together – in one package. It is not that the more we suffer the more we know him; it's just that suffering is part of the deal. Paul actually wrote to Timothy, stating that, "Indeed, all who desire to live a godly life in Christ Jesus will be persecuted." (2.Tim.3:12)

Baker's New Testament commentary also says that…

> *Paul yearns to participate more and more fully in the reproaches and afflictions of his Lord and Saviour. He wants to "fill up whatever is lacking in the sufferings of Christ for his body, the Church".[1]*

Now that is an interesting verse! The phrase "fill up" is a very rare compound verb and is only used here. In the Greek language it is *antanaplērō*, which literally means 'to fill up in turn'. Robertson's Word Pictures puts in beautifully for me:

> *It is now Paul's 'turn' at the bat, to use a baseball figure. Christ had his 'turn', the grandest of all and suffered for us all in a sense not true of anyone else.[2]*

The "what is lacking" phrase simply means that there was a lot more to come, and that it was Paul's turn, and then that of those who followed, right down to us here today. In a very precious sense, as we take on the suffering that closeness to Christ often incurs, we find ourselves identifying with him. Dietrich Bonhoeffer once wrote:

> *A Christian is someone who shares the suffering of God in this world.[3]*

Thought

If we follow him closely, then whatever is aimed at him will surely hit us.

---

[1] *Baker's New Testament Commentary,* e-sword.net, with quote from Col.1:24
[2] *Robertson's Word Pictures,* e-sword.net
[3] http://www.azquotes.com/author/1638-Dietrich_Bonhoeffer/tag/suffering

Prayer

Do not let me miss the deepest thing Thou hast to give ... the fellowship of Thy sufferings.[1]

---

[1]   Frank Houghton, Amy Carmichael of Dohnavur, (SPCL, London, 1953), p.311

DAY FIFTY-FIVE

Patience and Impatient

Phil.3:8-11

Indeed, I count everything as loss because of the surpassing worth of knowing Christ Jesus my Lord. For his sake I have suffered the loss of all things and count them as rubbish, in order that I may gain Christ and be found in him, not having a righteousness of my own that comes from the law, but that which comes through faith in Christ, the righteousness from God that depends on faith – that I may know him and the power of his resurrection, and may share his sufferings, becoming like him in his death, that by any means possible I may attain the resurrection from the dead.

Today, I want to think about three words: "becoming like him". Spiritual theology talks about 'union with Christ'. This is far deeper than knowing about him, or even having the occasional spiritual experience of him. Rather, this is the entering into a union at the deepest levels possible with him, where our hearts and spirits are one with his. Desmond Tillyer, writing of the teachings of St John of the Cross, in his little book *Union with God*, said:

> *What we are being led to is an intimate knowledge of God which is deeper than thoughts and words, concepts and ideas, and therefore remains inexpressible, beyond comprehension, and yet totally penetrating and transforming the soul.[1]*

Paul was seeking this oneness with Jesus. The phrase "becoming like him" (ESV/NIV), "being conformed" (NASB) is the one Greek word *summorphizomenos*. It properly means 'to be conformed inwardly in one's experience to something, to assimilate into oneself the life or experience of another'. It is also found, in another form, in Rom 8:29, where Paul wrote about being "predestined to be conformed to the image of his Son". The word describes "an inward and not merely superficial

---

[1] Desmond Tillyer, *Union with God,* (Mowbray, London, 1984), p.18

conformity"[1]. Becoming like Jesus was his life's goal. Kenneth Wuest described this deep, persistent desire of Paul as a seeking of "conformity to the spirit and temper of His life, the meekness, lowliness, and the submission of Christ"[2]. This was more than powerful ministry; this was likeness. This was Christlikeness, and at the deepest levels.

When I was a young associate pastor in London in the mid 70's, I was asked to pick up a Bulgarian pastor from a hotel in order to bring him to one of our meetings. His name was Haralan Popov, and he had been imprisoned and tortured in Communist prisons and concentration camps for 13 years because of his faith in Christ. They had treated him horrifically. Marie Notcheva, a Christian writer and certified biblical counselor from Massachusetts, wrote of Haralan:

> For several weeks, the pastor was brutally beaten, starved, and forced to stand motionless staring point-blank at a shiny white wall for days at a time.[3]

The torture increased over the years, but his faith in, and love for, Jesus also increased.

As I entered the hotel, I noticed him, a small, almost diminutive man, who sat in the corner of the entrance hall. After a few words, I escorted him to my car. We spoke very little, but I began to become aware of something like a strong spiritual fragrance filling the car as we drove. It came from within him. This dear man was exuding the fragrant presence of Christ. I have never forgotten it. It seemed that they were becoming one with each other.

Thought

In all my interactions today, will I remind people of Christ?

Prayer

Lord, please draw me into such a deeper relationship with you so that I start to resemble you in my conversations and relationships with those around me.

---

[1]   *Robertson's Word Pictures,* e-sword.net
[2]   Kenneth Wuest, *Philippians, Word Studies in the Greek New Testament, Vol.2,* (Eerdmans, Michigan, 1942), p.94
[3]   https://marienotcheva.wordpress.com/2015/10/20/review-tortured-for-his-faith-by-haralan-popov

DAY FIFTY-SIX

Conforming to His Death

Phil.3:8-11

Indeed, I count everything as loss because of the surpassing worth of knowing Christ Jesus my Lord. For his sake I have suffered the loss of all things and count them as rubbish, in order that I may gain Christ and be found in him, not having a righteousness of my own that comes from the law, but that which comes through faith in Christ, the righteousness from God that depends on faith – that I may know him and the power of his resurrection, and may share his sufferings, becoming like him in his death, that by any means possible I may attain the resurrection from the dead.

We are not talking about finding a literal whip to be scourged with, a literal cross to be crucified on, and a literal tomb where we are buried in and resurrected from. Instead, we mean the very spirit and tenor of the life of Christ, who laid down his own life in order that we might live. Christ died for sin, and we too must die to sin. Jesus gave up his life for others, and we must adopt the same mindset. In two very moving passages, (Ex.32:30-32 / Rom.9:1-3) we read that both Paul and Moses were willing to not only lose their own lives, but also lose their place and salvation with God for the sake of the people of God. This demonstrated such a depth of sacrificial love for the people of God that it cuts us to the quick.

In sharp contrast, our lives can be so full of self-preservation and self-fulfilment. Hear what Paul wrote to the Corinthians: "I will most gladly spend and be spent for your souls." (2.Cor.12:15) The word "spent" he used was *ekdapanaō*, and meant 'to be all spent out to the point of exhausting all my resources'. Here was evidence of a totally unselfish life.

This is yet another of Paul's great themes. Of himself he writes, "I have been crucified with Christ," (Gal.2:20) and of others he writes, "You have died, and your life is hid with Christ in God." (Col.3:3). Death must be at work in us if we are to be truly authentic in our walk with Christ. Jesus said, "Listen carefully: Unless a grain of wheat is buried in the ground, dead to the world, it is never any more than a grain of wheat.

But if it is buried, it sprouts and reproduces itself many times over. In the same way, anyone who holds on to life just as it is destroys that life. But if you let it go, reckless in your love, you'll have it forever, real and eternal." (Jn.12:24,25, The Message) The New Living Translation (NLT) renders it this way: "Those who love their life in this world will lose it. Those who care nothing for their life in this world will keep it for eternity."

Paul took this particular dimension of walking with Christ seriously. To the believers in Corinth, he wrote, "For I decided to know nothing among you except Jesus Christ and him crucified." (1.Cor.2:2) He also wrote to the Galatian believers, "And those who belong to Christ Jesus have crucified the flesh with its passions and desires." (Gal.5:24) "But far be it from me to boast except in the cross of our Lord Jesus Christ, by which the world has been crucified to me, and I to the world." (Gal.6:14) Maybe that is what Jesus meant when he said that if we wanted to follow him, then we too would have to pick up our cross. It's not just an event; it's a way of life.

Thomas à Kempis wrote these deeply challenging words:

> *Jesus has always many who love his heavenly kingdom, but few who bear his cross. He has many who desire consolation, but few who care for trial. He finds many to share his table, but few to take part in his fasting. All desire to be happy with him; few wish to suffer anything for him.*[1]

Thought

In the spiritual life, death is a prelude to life – daily, and in all dimensions.

Prayer

Lord, help me to embrace the cross, and not fight it. May death do its work in me so that your life might, through me, become even more apparent.

---

[1]   Thomas à Kempis, *The Imitation of Christ,* (Hendrickson, Massachusetts, 2004), p.47

DAY FIFTY-SEVEN

Say What You Mean

Phil.3:8-11

Indeed, I count everything as loss because of the surpassing worth of knowing Christ Jesus my Lord. For his sake I have suffered the loss of all things and count them as rubbish, in order that I may gain Christ and be found in him, not having a righteousness of my own that comes from the law, but that which comes through faith in Christ, the righteousness from God that depends on faith – that I may know him and the power of his resurrection, and may share his sufferings, becoming like him in his death, that by any means possible I may attain the resurrection from the dead.

Death is always part of the authentic Christian experience – the dying to self, the laying down of our lives for the benefit of others, even for those we find unlovely and ungrateful. God did it, and he calls us to do the same. In another passage that is full of unbelievable depth, Paul writes, "But we have this treasure in jars of clay, to show that the surpassing power belongs to God and not to us. We are afflicted in every way, but not crushed; perplexed, but not driven to despair; persecuted, but not forsaken; struck down, but not destroyed; always carrying in the body the death of Jesus, so that the life of Jesus may also be manifested in our bodies. For we who live are always being given over to death for Jesus' sake, so that the life of Jesus also may be manifested in our mortal flesh. So death is at work in us, but life in you." (2.Cor.4:7-12) This is Christianity at its finest!

Kenneth Wuest captures it beautifully, writing:

Paul desires the full operation of this life to surge through his Christian experience in such a manner that the fragrance of the life of his Lord may permeate his life. This is the goal to which he is striving and the goal to which he has not yet attained.[1]

Paul now moves on to talk about "the attaining of the resurrection from the dead", and he wants to attain this by "any means possible". The word "resurrection" is actually *exanastasin*, and it is only found here. It literally means 'out-resurrection'. This is a difficult passage, and I see two lines of thought here, both of them beautiful and deeply challenging. In the first instance, Paul is referring to a powerful outworking of God's inclusive work in Christ as seen in Eph.2:4-8: "...but God, being rich in mercy, because of the great love with which he loved us, even when we were dead in our trespasses, made us alive together with Christ – by grace you have been saved – and raised us up with him and seated us with him in the heavenly places in Christ Jesus..." We are called to exhibit, not only the fragrance of the crucified Christ, but also the unbelievable power of the risen Christ. We were recreated for victory. It has been put it this way: Paul desired "to be raised completely above sin and selfishness, so that he could be a most effective agent for the salvation of men to the glory of God"[2].

Secondly, Paul is thinking as well about the resurrection from the dead of all believers, those who have been forgiven, washed clean by the blood of the lamb, and who will stand before him, seeing him clearly, knowing him in full, and free from all the restrictions of their old natures. This is not just resurrection – this is absolute transformation. Let me imagine a little: this will be the ability to see and perceive with breathless wonder the unspeakable beauty and glory of the Father, Son and Holy Spirit; the ability to run and never be weary, where ageing and weakness is unknown. It was for this that Paul ached. This was the deepest longing of his heart.

Thought

Father of Jesus, love's reward, what rapture will it be!
Prostrate before Thy throne to lie, and gaze and gaze on Thee![3]

---

[1]   Kenneth Wuest, *Philippians,* Word Studies in the Greek New Testament, *Vol.2,* (Eerdmans, Michigan, 1942), p.94
[2]   *Baker's New Testament Commentary,* e-sword.net
[3]   Frederick William Faber, *My God, how wonderful Thou art,* (Kingsway, Eastbourne, 2003)

Prayer

Dear Lord, please make this the focus and the deepest desire of my heart.

Day Fifty-Eight

Take Initiative in your Responses

Phil.3:12

*Not that I have already obtained this or am already perfect,
but I press on to make it my own, because Christ Jesus has
made me his own.*

Let's recap the fivefold desires of Paul concerning his walk with Christ. Firstly, and above all, he wanted to know Jesus deeply and personally. For him, all roads had to lead here. To know Jesus must also be our personal and passionate desire, as it was Paul's. Secondly, he wanted to experience Jesus' power, firstly in his own life, and then through him into the lives of others. Thirdly, he wanted to know and share in his suffering, rejoicing that it was his turn to take the knocks that came with identifying ourselves fully with Christ. Fourthly, he wanted to know Christ's death, being willing to die to his own desires and lay down his own life for others on a daily basis. Fifthly, he wanted to know that extraordinary 'out-resurrection', finding himself unhindered and victorious in his personal walk, and longing for the day when he would be seeing and serving his Lord with no restrictions whatsoever.

Paul had such strong desires and high ideals, and he longed for better things, but he was no idealistic dreamer who lived in an almost fantasy world of super-spirituality. Paul yearned for and aimed at a profound experience of Christ, but also realised that he had a very long way to go on the journey. Here, too, is the tension that we live in. We have been saved, and we are also being saved. We have been made whole, and we are also being made whole. The more Paul saw of Christ, the more he realised that he, Paul, was actually quite imperfect and had not yet arrived. In fact, the nearer we ourselves get to him, the more we will sense our own imperfections and shortcomings. The brighter the light is, the more we will notice our own inner darkness and shadows.

I am reminded of the prophet Isaiah, who upon seeing the Lord said: "Woe is me, I am undone." (Isa.6:5) That can also be translated, "I am reduced to silence…" In almost all the biblical encounters with the divine, the immediate reaction was fearfulness, and the angel had to say, "Fear not..." Annie Dillard wrote:

> *It is madness to wear ladies' straw hats and velvet hats to church; we should all be wearing crash helmets. Ushers should issue life preservers and signal flares; they should lash us to our pews. For the sleeping god may wake someday and take offense, or the waking god may draw us out to where we can never return.*[1]

The phrase "obtained it" could be better translated 'made it my own experience'. The word Paul used was *elabon*, which means 'to take, and lay hold of with the hand'. He was saying, "Concerning my dream of intense closeness, intimacy and identification with Christ, I have seen it, but I have not yet fully grasped it." Paul also says that he is not "perfect". The word he used there was *teteleiōmai*, and it meant 'to be fully developed', not in the sense of being sinless or flawless, but in the sense of having a fully developed spiritual maturity. Paul was growing, but he was not yet fully grown up. He knew that he was not there yet – there was still room for development and progress.

It is sad to see those who feel that they have 'arrived', who feel that there is nothing more to learn, no new avenues to explore, and no new areas to be stretched into. You see, when we lose our stretchability, we become like an old wineskin, and we become a liability rather than a blessing to the church.

Thought

It is a good thing to keep your 'learner' plates on all the way through your life.

Prayer

Dear Lord, please help me to have a realistic view of my walk with you today.

---

[1] Annie Dillard, *Teaching a Stone to Talk,* (Harper & Row, New York, 1982), pp.40,41.

DAY FIFTY-NINE

Apprehending

Phil.3:12

Not that I have already obtained this or am already perfect, but I press on to make it my own, because Christ Jesus has made me his own.

Yesterday, we noticed that in verse 13, Paul had stated again that he had "not arrived", and that he had also used the phrase "I do not consider". The word that he used here was *logizomai*, and it meant 'to carefully consider'. It carried with it a sense of thoughtful consideration, as opposed to a momentary emotional and temporary response. It was the result of deep and careful reflection.

Neither was it that negative mindset that says, "I can never get there." That, to Paul, would have been pure defeatism. Paul was making a careful, sustained and honest appraisal of his spiritual progress; a mark of a true and genuine humility.

Paul wrote, "I press on to make it my own." It can be translated more literally 'I pursue this', and it spoke of a long and prolonged pursuit, a lifetime spent hunting down the dream. Paul wasn't about to throw in the towel! This speaks most powerfully to the postmodern and consumerist mindsets of today, which pursue things for a little while, until they get bored with the journey and even the goal, and then turn aside for something more immediate and satisfying.

Paul was pressing on; he was pursuing to "make it [his] own". This was interesting language. The phrase he used here was the one word *katalambanō*. We came across the word *lambano* in verse 12, which meant 'to take by the hand'. Here, however, we have the prefix *kata*, which meant 'down'. It can be thus translated 'to take hold of, pulling it down'. Imagine a rugby tackle. We see the ball in the hands of another player, and we go off after him in a hot and sustained pursuit, in order to pull him down to grab the ball.

Christians can be rather vague at times about their goals in life. Whenever asked, "What are you pursuing or chasing after?" the answers given are often unclear. Paul, on the other hand, was crystal clear: he wanted to know Christ in his fullness, and he wanted that fullness to be manifested in and through him. Vagueness of vision will cripple any forward movement. Without a vision "people perish"[1], "cast off restraint"[2]. In other words, they wander aimlessly through their lives, hoping to arrive into heaven. To use again the analogy of the rugby game, there are some people who are just running around the field, enjoying the atmosphere of the game, whilst there are a few who are chasing after the ball. We need to see that there is something in life that is worth pursuing, and then we need to go for it, pursue it, with all of our might. And it is usually the 'one thing' that we pursue, that is caught. Chase many dreams and we can end up chasing our tail.

When we remember what Paul had written up to this point, we need to remember that he had 'dumped' a lot of stuff in order to pursue the one thing. He was now running unimpeded, and so should we.

Thought

It is the people of the 'one thing' that go the furthest and make the deepest impact.

Prayer

Dear God, help me to unclutter my life, so that I can see more clearly where I should, in fact, be headed.

---

[1]   Proverbs 29:18 (KJV)
[2]   Ibid. (ESV)

DAY SIXTY

The Prayer of Faith

Phil.3:12

Not that I have already obtained this or am already perfect, but I press on to make it my own, because Christ Jesus has made me his own.

I'm taking time with this particular passage of Scripture because it is so rich in meaning. There is so much truth here that is vital for our Christian walk. A cursory reading of the Bible will give you a big picture, but study and meditation will yield much more. Do not merely skim the surface of Scripture, but learn to dig deep. You will need to invest time to do so, but the results will be rewarding and life-changing.

Paul was in hot pursuit of his vision – his dream – of walking closely with Jesus, entering into such a depth of relationship with him that it became manifest in his own life. He was using the language of the Greek games. He had entered a race with the prize in his sights and was not going to simply amble along the track, taking in the sights and the atmosphere. Fire had entered his soul, resulting in a passion that would run hard, producing sweat until he overtook and captured his goal.

Paul wrote, "I press on…" The word he used was *diōkō*, and it meant 'to pursue, to chase swiftly, to persecute'. There was an intensity about this word; this was no casual relationship where he could take it or leave it. He had a deep and strong desire to be always just behind the shoulder of the Lord, so that whenever Jesus glanced around, there he would be in hot pursuit, running and walking at Jesus' pace, following his direction. There was this sense of a dogged, steady and persistent pursuit in Paul's language, almost a 'shadowing' of the Lord.

All this was because, in the first place, he has been apprehended himself by Christ. The same word, *katalambanō*, was used. Jesus had chased after him and 'wrestled him to the ground' as he had approached Damascus. John Gill, one of the finest nineteenth century commentators put it this way:

[Paul] was apprehended of Christ, when he met him in his way to Damascus, stopped him in his journey, laid him prostrate

*on the ground, and laid hold on him as his own, challenged
and claimed his interest in him, as one that the Father had
given him, and he had purchased by his blood; he entered into
him, and took possession of him, and took up his residence in
him.[1]*

Paul, the one who had been in hot pursuit of Christians, actually found himself being hotly pursued and apprehended by the Lord Jesus.

Paul was now chasing after a personal relationship with Jesus, because Jesus was chasing after a personal relationship with Paul. But there was also a purpose to the relationship. Why did Jesus wrestle Paul to the ground? And what was Paul seeking to wrestle to the ground? The NASB has the text, "...that I may lay hold of that for which also I was laid hold of by Christ Jesus." The Lord shared that purpose with a man called Ananias: "He is a chosen instrument of mine to carry my name before the Gentiles and kings and the children of Israel..." (Acts 9:15) We need to ask ourselves, why am I here at this time in this place; why did Jesus get hold of me? He did so because he wanted me to walk with him for a specific purpose. He wants us to walk closely with him, with a holy passion, becoming like him in character and also in ministry.

Thought

What does it mean to "carry [his] name"? It means to be a "personal representative"[2].

Prayer

Lord Jesus, I am yours. You have conquered me. Let me represent you well today.

---

[1] *John Gill's Exposition of the Whole Bible*, e-sword.net
[2] MSG

DAY SIXTY-ONE

The Power of Confession

Phil.3:13

Brothers, I do not consider that I have made it my own. But one thing I do: forgetting what lies behind and straining forward to what lies ahead...

Imagine the athlete with his feet in the blocks, ready to run the marathon. What do you think is in his mind? Any athlete will tell you that the success of the race is determined mainly by the frame of mind that he or she is in. The mindset is everything.

There seems to me, however, to be two extremes. The first is a false humility and the other is an overconfidence. The first says, "I could never do this," and the second says, "Whatever I do, it's a cinch." The truth is that we cannot do all that we want to do, but we can certainly do all that he asks us to do. He will empower us to do all that he requires of us. This race, by God's grace, can be run; and this race, by God's grace, can be won. Thus, Paul had a certain frame of mind in his pursuit of intimacy and identification with Christ.

He also had a sharp focus. He wrote, "This one thing I do." In the Greek it was just two words: "one thing". It reminds me of its counterpart in the Old Testament. David, in Psa.27:4 writes, "One thing have I asked of the LORD, that will I seek after: that I may dwell in the house of the LORD all the days of my life, to gaze upon the beauty of the LORD, and to inquire in his temple." You, know, some would consider that a waste of time...

A literal reading of Heb.12:1 would be, 'We must deliberately lift our eyes away from the things that easily distract us, and focus instead with a complete concentration on him – and continue doing so.' This, then, is a persistent and determined concentration. Some people, however, do love the distractions, and they are the ones who never win races.

The athlete has one thing in mind: the winning of the race and the grasping of the prize. Paul wrote to the Corinthians, "Do you not know that in a race all the runners run, but only one receives the prize? So run that you may obtain it." (1.Cor.9:24) The word "obtain" is that word *katalambanō*, which meant 'to pursue to grasp and pull down.'

How did he run? Very simply, he completely forgot what lay behind him. How many runners have lost because they glanced behind? In 1954 there was a world-famous mile race in Vancouver between Roger Bannister and John Landy. They were the only two who had run a mile in under four minutes. On the home stretch, Landy could not hear Bannister's feet pounding behind him and so he looked back, and Bannister surged past him to win the race. Paul refused to glance back at what he had been. Remember also Lot's wife. Remember, too, the words of Jesus: "No one who puts his hand to the plough and looks back is fit for the kingdom of God." (Lk.9:32)

Next, he used the words "straining forward to what lies ahead". The word "straining" is a different word to that of "pressing on". It is *epekteinomai*, and it means 'to stretch oneself forward'. If you like, he was running like a dog straining at the leash. This was no mid-afternoon, laid-back ramble with the Lord – this was a full on, flat out, dogged, stretched-out determination to win the race. May it be so also with us!

Thought

'Pursuit', 'longing', 'hungering and thirsting' – these are key words of the kingdom.

Prayer

Dear Lord, deliver me from the soul-numbing boredom of this present age.

DAY SIXTY-TWO

The Power of Prayer

Phil.3:14

...I press on toward the goal for the prize of the upward call of God in Christ Jesus.

In this walk with Christ, there is a time to remember and a time to forget. We need to remember the good and forget the bad. Paul was determined not to be crippled by his past. He wrote that he was "forgetting what lies behind..." Many people, on their journey with Christ, have been stunted and held back by past events. Kenneth Wuest wrote that the word "forgetting" was stronger than merely 'forgetting'; it meant "completely forgetting"[1]. Chris Short, one of my first mentors into leadership, used to tell me each time I failed at something to "repent, rejoice and press on!" That good advice still rings in my ears.

Twice in the passage we find the phrase "press[ing] on..." and we remind ourselves that the words meant 'to swiftly run after'. It carried a sense of 'persecuting' or 'harassing'. Paul had this dream of being like Christ and he pursued it like a heat-seeking missile.

We also remind ourselves that his language was that of the Greek Games. St Anthony of Egypt, the founder of the Desert Fathers, in describing those who pursued a close walk with Christ, coined the phrase *'Athletai Dei'* – 'Athletes of God'. This involved training, discipline and a sharp focus. Paul wrote to the Corinthians, "Every athlete in training submits to strict discipline, in order to be crowned with a wreath that will not last; but we do it for one that will last forever." (1.Cor.9:25, GNB) Chrysostom wrote:

> *He that runs looks not at the spectators, but at the prize. He is not easily distracted.*[2]

Paul talked of "the goal". The word used here was *skopos*, and it is only found here. It meant 'a distant mark that is looked at, the end goal

---

[1] Kenneth Wuest, *Word Studies in the Greek New Testament, Vol 2, Philippians,* (Eerdmans, Michigan, 1970), p.97
[2] Cited in *Vincent's Word Studies,* e-sword.net

in view'. Classical Greek used the word to describe 'a mark for shooting at'. It has the prefix *kata* – 'down' – and therefore gives the sense of bearing down on a goal. It also meant 'according to', and thereby described a race shaped and determined by its goal. If we are merely on a spiritual ramble through life, we shall be shaped and directed by all sorts of things; if, on the other hand, we are running a race like Paul, we will be people of the "one thing" – shaped by the one goal.

He then mentioned "the prize". The word here was *brabeion*, and it was derived from the word *brabeus* – 'an umpire'. Paul had in mind here the prize of a crown. He wrote to Timothy, "I have fought the good fight, I have finished the race, I have kept the faith. Henceforth there is laid up for me the crown of righteousness, which the Lord, the righteous judge, will award to me on that Day, and not only to me but also to all who have loved his appearing." (2.Tim.4:7,8)

There is a difference between "the goal" and "the prize". The first speaks of our determined and focused efforts here on the earth, and the second speaks of the gift and reward of God that will come to us as we stand before him on that last day. I don't know about you, but I want to hear from his lips, "Well done, good and faithful servant... You fought the fight, you finished the race and you kept the faith... Enter now into the joy of heaven."

Thought

There is a huge difference between taking a stroll in the park and running a marathon.

Prayer

Dear Lord, help me to focus today on my main calling – to become like you.

DAY SIXTY-THREE

The Upward Call

Phil.3:14

...I press on toward the goal for the prize of the upward call of God in Christ Jesus.

Goal-setting is an important part of living an effective life. We often joke about the little saying, 'Aim at nothing, and you'll be sure to hit it!' but it's true! In the spiritual walk, however, there is the one goal, and out of that one goal there are what I would call subsidiary goals. For the Christian, the one goal, the primary and life-shaping goal, is simply this: to be like Jesus in word and deed, in thought and response. Drift from this and I believe we will weaken our subsidiary goals: to be better in our giftings and functions; our relationships; our effectiveness.

Paul had been gripped with such a high calling, and it had never left him. Jesus had apprehended, captured and arrested him with a calling to become an ambassador, a representative of the kingdom of heaven, here on the earth. This was a high calling – and not merely a calling to be an apostle. It was a calling to walk with, imitate and serve the Lord Jesus Christ. If we truly understand Paul's understanding of calling in his letters, it is clear to see that is the same for every saint. We are all called to walk with, know deeply and intimately, and reflect accurately Christ in the earth.

This call has direction to it. We have mentioned the forward movement of this call but let me refer to the upward direction. J. Hugh Michael, in his commentary writes:

Paul heard God's call at his conversion, and through the intervening years it had not ceased to summon him upwards.[1]

This call, then, is from heaven and it directs us towards heaven. This call has built into it a power from heaven to draw us, shape us and lead us.

---

[1]   J. Hugh Michael, *The Epistle of Paul to the Philippians,* (Hodder & Stoughton, London, 1954), p.163

Let's be honest here: in each one of us is a basic nature that has an inbuilt 'downward drag'. Some, quite frankly, are not bothered by this and just put it down to human nature – which it is. Others, on the other hand, are deeply concerned about this and seek to submit themselves to the inward cleansing and empowering work of the Holy Spirit. This upward call of God 'mitigates' and strives against this default, this downward drag in us. If you like, the Holy Spirit is always reinforcing this upward call by insisting that we always step up to a higher level of living. The Holy Spirit said to the exiled John the apostle on Patmos, "Come up here," and the apostle was shown vision after vision of life in heaven. The Holy Spirit is still saying this. Such visions are designed to purify us and focus us.

This call is really a summons, and not merely an invitation. It is more like an impelling command, but it has also within it an empowering element. There is a draw and a pull from heaven and also a push towards heaven. It comes to us with authority, impelling us to respond. It speaks deeply within us to live in Christ – because this is the primary sphere that we are called to. Other spheres of service are secondary. So, here it is. The high calling on your life is this: Jesus has come to you, and he says, "Walk with me – closely – at a higher level. Let my life, thoughts and ways shape yours, and out of this relationship, reflect me accurately to those around you."

Thought

Understand the magnitude of the call of God on your life, and things will change.

Prayer

Dear Lord, please emphasise again to me my primary calling – which is to know you.

DAY SIXTY-FOUR

Mature Thought

Phil.3:15

Let those of us who are mature think this way, and if in anything you think otherwise, God will reveal that also to you.

We can easily put Paul on a pedestal, thinking that his walk with Christ is quite beyond our reach. That can be quite convenient for us, because we end up thinking that we are not really obliged to imitate him. Paul, however, did not let us off the hook that easily. His use of the "I" in verses 12-14 turned into the "us" in verse 15 where he wrote, "Let those of us who are mature think this way..." In verse 17, he wrote quite explicitly, "Brothers, join in imitating me..." The word used here, and only here, was *sunmimētai*, which meant 'join together in imitating [me]'. Bishop Lightfoot put it this way: "Vie with each other in imitating me."[1] In other words, Paul was saying, "In the same way, with the same focus and passion that I imitate Christ, all of you imitate me." He also wrote to the Corinthian believers, "I urge you, then, be imitators of me," (1.Cor.4:16) and again, "Be imitators of me, as I am of Christ." (1.Cor.11:1)

Paul's example, then, is the norm for all believers. This is not just for apostles and prophets, pastors and teachers and evangelists – it is for all of us who have committed ourselves to following Jesus, and the standards are high. In 1957, a Chinese pastor called Watchman Nee wrote a powerful book called *The Normal Christian Life*. In its first chapter, describing this 'normal Christian life', he wrote:

> *...it is something very different from the life of the ordinary Christian.*[2]

Let us be clear about this: our faith was never designed to be a mere appendix to our life; it was designed to consume us and transform us from being "mere men" (1.Cor.3:3, NASB) to extraordinary people.

---

[1] Cited in *Robertson's Word Pictures*, e-sword.net
[2] Watchman Nee, *The Normal Christian Life*, (Victory Press, London, 1961), p.9

148

There are two thoughts here that I want to draw out. Firstly, Paul made a comment about spiritual maturity. The word can mean 'grown up'. There is always room for further growth, but we have passed a marker – we are now no longer children. We, too, have to make this transition if we are going to go on with Christ. We are exhorted to be childlike in our faith and innocence, but not childish in our conversation and behaviour. There is a huge difference between the two.

Secondly, Paul commented on the thought life of the believers. He wrote, "Think this way." The NASB puts it this way: "Have this attitude." Paul actually used this turn of phrase ten times in this letter, so it was an important issue to him. We need to determine the content of our thoughts, because regular thought patterns become habitual. For Paul, spiritual maturity was evidenced in thinking along certain paths. His challenges to us today are clear: if we are not pursuing Christ, seeking to live as close as we can to him, reflecting his life through our words and deeds, then we haven't grown up. Children and youth pursue their own interests. Maturity seeks the interests of Christ. If we are not pursuing Christ, seeking to grow and develop in Christ-like character, seeking his interests, then we should not be in any form of leadership. Mark this: it will never be simply our words that affect people; it will be the way we live out our lives before them – in public and also in the home. Therefore, to seek to be like Paul, who himself sought to be like Christ, is spiritual maturity.

Thought

When Paul used the words "mere men", it was not a compliment.

Prayer

Father, help me to make the transition between a spiritual adolescence to real maturity.

DAY SIXTY-FIVE

Holding True

Phil.3:16

Only let us hold true to what we have attained.

Spiritual maturity is evidenced mainly by a passionate desire to imitate the life of Christ. Thomas à Kempis wrote in the first chapter of his powerful little book *The Imitation of Christ* that…

> *…we are advised to imitate His life and habits, if we wish to be truly enlightened and free from all blindness of heart. Let our chief effort, therefore, be to study the life of Jesus Christ.[1]*

This was Paul's lifelong goal and pursuit, and he insisted that is should be for all believers as well. Peterson put it this way in the Message: "So, let's keep focused on that goal, those of us who want everything God has for us. If any of you have something else in mind, something less than total commitment, God will clear your blurred vision – you'll see it yet!" Any vision less than a total commitment to the likeness of Christ is a blurred vision.

Paul then moved on to what seemed like a moment of evaluation. He wrote, "Only let us hold true to what we have attained." The word "attained" here was not the same word translated "attained" in 3:12. There, it meant 'taking it by the hand and making it my own experience'. Here, however, it meant 'to direct one's life, to live, to anticipate arriving'. The Expanded Translation has it: "Only one thing, so far as we have come, let us keep our lives in the same path." Here, then, was a call to unity, not of doctrine as much, but of direction and focus. None of us have full light on everything, and so, to quote Ralph Martin:

> *Until you have fuller light, be content to be open minded and teachable, and guide your life by the light you have received.[2]*

---

[1]   Thomas à Kempis, *The Imitation of Christ,* Book 1, (Hendrickson, Massachusetts, 2004), p.3

[2]   Ralph P. Martin, *The Epistle of Paul to the Philippians,* (The Tyndale Press, London, 1963), p.156

Albert Barnes added another facet to this when he wrote:

> *The meaning is this, that though there might be different degrees of attainment among Christians, and different views on many subjects, yet there were points in which all could agree; there were attainments which they all had made, and in reference to them they should walk in harmony and love.*[1]

Wherever we are at in our Christian walk, this one goal should unite us: we want to be like Christ. Wherever we are, we should be thinking in this same direction.

The Preacher's Commentary states:

> *We may state this truth in another way, which applies to each of us, no matter where we are on our journey. Fidelity to truth already attained is a condition of receiving further and fuller truth.*[2]

Here, the emphasis is on staying true to what we have learnt. I have two thoughts here. The first is that divine truth comes to us "line upon line, precept upon precept". (Isa.28:13) In our scramble for new things, we must never abandon what we have learnt. According to Christ, "Then you see how every student well-trained in God's kingdom is like the owner of a general store who can put his hands on anything you need, old or new, exactly when you need it."(Matt.13:52, The Message) The second thought is this: it is only when we are walking in the revelation that we have received that more will open up to us. If there is no weight of experience and obedience to act as ballast, then the hot air of pure revelation will take us so high into the stratosphere that the balloon will burst, and the consequences will not be pretty.

Thought

In our pursuit for the new, never let us forget what we have already learnt.

Prayer

Dear Lord, help me to realise afresh that I am not the final authority on everything.

---

[1] Cited in http://biblehub.com/commentaries/barnes/philippians/3.htm
[2] *The Preacher's Commentary,* e-sword.net

DAY SIXTY-SIX

Modelling

Phil.3:17

Brothers, join in imitating me, and keep your eyes on those who walk according to the example you have in us.

When Paul wrote these words, it was to a group of people who had never seen or heard of Jesus Christ. News did not travel fast in those days. Philippi didn't even have a synagogue where the Old Testament scriptures were taught. All Paul found was a little prayer meeting among some women down by the river. (Acts 16:13) Words, then, were never going to be enough. There had to be a modelling before them of the life of Christ. Paul used a phrase that is only found here: *sunmimētai mou*, which literally meant 'be together followers of me'. We need to be precise here: he did not write, "Be followers together with me of Christ," but he wrote, "Join together in following me." This was not from any sense of arrogance; this was of necessity. These people had no idea of who Jesus was, what he had done and what he was like, and so Paul said, in effect, "Watch and learn from how I do life – then you'll get a pretty good idea of what Jesus is like."

Paul was not perfect, but he was certainly passionate about knowing Jesus deeply. It was as if Paul told the believers, "If you want to know how to live according to Christ, then follow my example."

I believe it can be a cop out to say, "Don't look at me; look at Jesus." In today's society, we are not too far away from that first century society, where there was little or no knowledge of Christ; hence there is a strong need today to model what we preach.

Paul encouraged the believers, not only to imitate him, but also to imitate those who walked according to the pattern that had been set by him. Others were imitating the Christ who lived in Paul in the same way that Paul was seeking to imitate Christ. The word "imitate" comes from the Greek word *tupon*, and it meant, 'a mark; an indentation that has been left behind'. Sometime later, the author of the letter to the Hebrews would write, "Remember your leaders, those who spoke to you the word of God. Consider the outcome of their way of life, and imitate their faith." (Heb.13:7) In other words, look at what has emerged from their lives; look at the fruit they have left behind them, and look at what remains in their trail.

Today, we have the Gospels and the letters of the apostles, and over two thousand years of outstanding examples of men and women who have walked a Christ-like life. It is well worth reading the biographies of these remarkable Christians in order to glean from their lives. We can ask the questions, what made them tick; how did they walk with the Lord; what were the secrets of their success? These are the men and women, marked by the Lord, and who themselves left a mark on the church and on society. We are foolish if we do not learn from them.

Here, then, are some huge personal challenges to us. What am I modelling to others? What am I leaving in my trail? What effect am I having on those around me? Am I an inspiration? Do I excite godliness and integrity to those I work with and live among? When it comes to the day of our funeral, what will men and women say of us in a few words? I once heard said, "What would you like to be said at your funeral? Write it down and make that your goal in life." I know what Paul's was: he wanted to walk closely to Christ.

Thought

Our living with the Lord should excite questions.

Prayer

Dear Lord, speak through, not only my words, but my actions today.

DAY SIXTY-SEVEN

Enemies of the Cross (1)

Phil.3:18

For many, of whom I have often told you and now tell you even with tears, walk as enemies of the cross of Christ.

Albert Schweitzer once wrote, "Example is not the main thing in influencing people – it is the only thing."[1] Paul sought to be a good example himself, and encouraged the noting and imitating of other good examples, and then went on to mention bad examples. We will experience both types of persons, and they will affect us, not so much by their words, but by the fruit of their words.

Most commentators feel that he was addressing a group of professing Christians who were still influenced by Epicurean and Antinomian tendencies – philosophies that devoted themselves to the modest satisfaction of the physical appetites and kicked against any moral law. For them, grace was a licence to please oneself; to indulge in pleasure but not in a harmful way.

Note how Paul spoke against them. There is a place for speaking negatively about people, but it is to be done in a way that is totally different to the world around us. It is with the intent of warning the saints and it is usually done with tears, on both sides. Paul wrote a tough letter to the church in Corinth: "For I wrote to you out of much affliction and anguish of heart and with many tears, not to cause you pain but to let you know the abundant love that I have for you." (2.Cor.2:4) His warnings went hand in hand with weeping. Let me pause here. Maybe the reason why we do not warn enough is because we do not love enough. Love sees ahead to the results of unbelieving and destructive behaviour, and it warns with feeling and tears.

Paul called these people "enemies of the cross of Christ". This is strong language. To understand this, we must first be clear about what the cross of Christ actually was. It was not a decorative piece to be worn or to put ornately into a church setting. It was, and is, an instrument of

---

[1] Albert Schweitzer, cited
    https://www.brainyquote.com/quotes/quotes/a/albertschw112973.html

death. People were crucified on a cross, and when Jesus called people to deny themselves and take up their cross, death to their own desires was uppermost in their minds. The cross of Christ does not adorn; it puts to death.

Who then, are these enemies of the cross? In the first instance, they seem to be those who professed to be believers in Christ. They were to be found within and around church life. To be blunt, they wanted all the benefits of the cross but not the cost. They wanted the destiny without the death. They desired the fruits of resurrection without the pain of the cross. We need to remember that there is no Easter Sunday without Good Friday. A.W. Tozer once wrote:

We want to be saved, but we insist that Christ does all the dying.[1]

To be an enemy of the cross is the natural thing to do. It is rooted in our basic nature. Nobody wants to die. Also, James wrote, "Do you not know that friendship with the world is enmity with God? Therefore whoever wishes to be a friend of the world makes himself an enemy of God." (Jas.4:4) To embrace the cross will put us on a collision course with the world and the worldly. Thomas à Kempis wrote:

Jesus has always many who love his heavenly kingdom, but few who bear his cross.[2]

Thought

An attitude of self-preservation is a huge hindrance to following the Saviour.

Prayer

Lord Jesus, help me to pick up the cross you bid me to carry.

---

[1]   A.W. Tozer, *The Root of the Righteous,* (Christian Publications, Harrisburg, 1955), p.66

[2]   Thomas à Kempis, *The Imitation of Christ,* Book 2, (Hendrickson, Massachusetts, 2004), p.47

Day Sixty-Eight

Enemies of the Cross (2)

Phil.3:19

Their end is destruction, their god is their belly, and they glory in their shame, with minds set on earthly things.

Once again, these are tough verses to look at and consider. It all seems such an alien culture to us living in the twenty-first century. This thought makes me want to pause here and say a word about teaching the word of God. Good exegesis will carefully examine the text, seeking to discover the exact meanings of the words and the context into which they were spoken. It will seek to recapture exactly what the original hearers heard in the first place. Then, good hermeneutics will seek to bring that same message right into the world in which we live, interpreting it so that we understand what was, and what is being said. So often, however, we bring our own hermeneutic to the text – our own way of seeing things. I believe that we must allow this timeless text to address us, to influence the way we think and interpret, and the way we do life. We must not bring our culture to the text; we bring the text to our culture. This kingdom is an eternal kingdom, with a culture of its own.

Paul wrote here of the "enemies of the cross", saying that "their end is destruction". The word he used was *apōleia*, which meant "not annihilation but ruination by separation from the presence of God"[1]. Baker's New Testament commentary says:

> *It does not mean that they will cease to exist. On the contrary, it means everlasting punishment (Matt.25:46), for this destruction is an everlasting destruction (2.Thess.1:9).[2]*

Alec Motyer wrote:

---

[1] Robert Lightner, *The Bible Knowledge Commentary,* edited by Walvoord and Zuck, (Victor Books, Illinois, 1983), p.662

[2] *Baker's New Testament Commentary,* e-sword.net

[Paul] looks beyond this world to the next and finds no hope at all for them there, nothing but eternal loss ... an eternal and irreversible separation from God.[1]

This was why Paul wept as he warned them.

He then wrote that "their god is their belly". This spoke of a devotion to self-indulgence. Their appetites and emotions were in control of their lives, and not subject to the discipline and rule of the Holy Spirit. Adam Clarke wrote:

They live not in any reference to eternity ... and live only to eat, drink, and be merry.[2]

When we live only for the moment, for the next gratifying experience, then we clearly reveal that we have not understood the way of Christ at all.

Paul went on to say that "they glory in their shame". Remember that he was addressing people in the vicinity of church life. Motyer wrote:

In other words, they exalt things and practices which they ought to be ashamed of but are not.[3]

The prophet Jeremiah called them people who had "forgotten how to blush". (Jer.6:15) This was an attitude that did not see any wrong in sinful ways and practices, and actually gloated about what they did. I would not like to be standing in their shoes on the final day. We have to live in the light of that day.

Lastly, Paul wrote that they "have their minds set on earthly things". This is a motif that is found throughout the New Testament, and it is never seen in a good light. If we are stuck with viewing the things of earth, then maybe we have never had a view of heaven, and therefore we need to examine ourselves to see if we really are in the faith. I carry a responsibility to ask that question.

Thought

We need to see the 'utter lostness' of the lost, to fully understand why Jesus died.

---

[1]   Alec Motyer, *The Message of Philippians,* (Inter-Varsity Press, Illinois, 1984), p.185

[2]   *Adam Clarke's Commentary on the Bible,* e-sword.net

[3]   Alec Motyer, *The Message of Philippians,* (Inter-Varsity Press, Illinois, 1984), p.185

Prayer

Father, please open my eyes to the fate of those who reject Jesus.

DAY SIXTY-NINE

Citizens of Heaven

Phil.3:20

*But our citizenship is in heaven, and from it we await a Savior,
the Lord Jesus Christ...*

In the last verse, we saw the characteristics of those who were enemies of the cross, possibly those who professed the Name of Christ, but whose lives were in violent contradiction to his ways. Paul says that their destiny was eternal destruction because they worshipped, not the Lord, but themselves. Their world view – their outlook on life – was purely natural and earthly.

He then brought about a sharp contrast and opened it up with a view of heaven. He reminded them, firstly, that their citizenship was in heaven. This was a word that his readers would readily understand. Philippi was a Roman colony – a miniature Rome if you like – and they were Roman citizens. They lived in Philippi but their citizenship was from Rome. In exactly the same manner, the believers lived in Philippi but their citizenship was in heaven. The phrase gave the sense of being fixed in heaven. Rome was transient and would one day fall. Heaven, on the other hand, is eternal. True believers are not rooted and grounded in something that will one day fade away or be usurped. The government of heaven is eternal. God reigns forever and ever. We are in Christ, sat with him in the heavens, before we are anywhere else. It is heaven that needs to fill our view, becoming, not only our base of operations, but the atmosphere in which we breathe.

Paul then went on to say that from this heaven, we await our Saviour. There is nothing and no one in this world that we can look to for our salvation. We do not look to this world to give us anything of spiritual value. Jesus is the one who came from heaven, accomplishing everything by his death and resurrection, and then he returned. Since then, churches have been established, acting as embassies of the kingdom of heaven, but even they are reliant on the life that flows from heaven. We, of ourselves, are not the answer. We are simply ambassadors who point as accurately as possible to the life of heaven.

The Greek word translated "await" was *apekdechometha*. It indicated an "earnest, patient waiting and expectation ... the compounded preposition apo denoted the withdrawal of attention from inferior objects"[1]. The intended sense was that of our attention withdrawn from all else, standing tiptoe in anticipation and longing for the return of Christ. Here there was focus, specific longings; and strong motivation. The biblical mindset is clear about this: we are "strangers and exiles here on the earth"; (Heb.11:13) we are people who "desire a better country, that is, a heavenly one"; (Heb.11:16) we are the people who have "come to Mount Zion and to the city of the living God, the heavenly Jerusalem, and to innumerable angels in festal gathering, and to the assembly of the firstborn who are enrolled in heaven, and to God, the judge of all, and to the spirits of the righteous made perfect, and to Jesus, the mediator of a new covenant..." (Heb.12:22-24)

Today, we await a Saviour, not to save us, but to transform us. He will transform our lowly bodies, that have been humiliated and stunted by the Fall, with all our faculties severely impeded and growing weaker and weaker through age and illness. When Jesus returns, however, the transformation will be into the likeness of his glorious body, unhindered, unimpeded; unrestricted. The glory that was lost by Adam's sin will be completely restored.

Thought

No longer rooted in the earth but rooted in heaven!

Prayer

Dear Lord, help me to see that my true nourishment comes from the things of heaven.

---

[1] *Vincent's Word Studies,* e-sword.net

DAY SEVENTY

Stand Firm

Phil.4:1

Therefore, my brothers, whom I love and long for, my joy and crown, stand firm thus in the Lord, my beloved.

Now we break into chapter 4 – well actually, we don't, because in the Greek text this verse actually finishes off the section we have been looking at in chapter 3. This is where the chapter and verse divisions in our Bible are not helpful; they sometimes break up prematurely the flow of the author's thoughts and intentions. A good clue for this is found in the little word "therefore". In other words, Paul finished off the section in the context of what he had just been writing.

Paul had said that that there were those, possibly on the fringes of the church, who were actually enemies of the cross, so intent on living for themselves. True believers, however, are to see themselves as citizens of an eternal and heavenly kingdom, influenced and shaped more by the eternal realms than by the temporal realms. In the light of that, we are waiting, almost impatiently, for the day when Jesus will come with an amazing personal transformational package for each one of us. In the light of these things, he said, "Don't give up, but stand firm instead." Persecution was beginning to bite, there were discouraging sights within their ranks, and some were being tempted to defect. One unknown writer said, "Standing firm is difficult when a panic starts…" But something wonderful is at work within us and something wonderful awaits us. Stand firm, therefore.

I love the terminology he used in describing these believers. They were his brothers – *adelphoi*. The term was fairly generic and could read 'brothers and sisters'. These people were family to him. When it comes to the church, the New Testament is awash with familial terminology: "brothers", "sisters", "mothers" and "fathers". For Paul, all these different people from their differing backgrounds had become a "family", and that is how we are to see and respond to each other. We are far more than members of the same church.

Paul's language was strong here. These people were also the *agapētoi* – 'the loved ones'. The phrase contained the *agapē* element. In other words, this was a love for them that is supernatural in its source, sacrificial in its nature and constant in its commitment. He also called them the *epipothētoi*, which meant 'the longed for ones'. This particular adjective was found only here in this form. Paul not only loved them, he yearned for them, wanting to see their faces, to be near them. When he was with them, his heart was refreshed and full. Such ardent and holy expressions are the foundation of a true and authentic ministry.

He also called them his "joy and crown". This was language similar to that which he used in describing the believers at Thessalonica: "For what is our hope or joy or crown of boasting before our Lord Jesus at his coming? Is it not you? For you are our glory and joy." (1.Thess.2:19,20). The word "joy" was *chara*, meaning 'cheer', 'delight', 'gladness'. These were the people whose very presence cheered him up and put heart back into him. They were his "crown" – his 'laurel wreath' – composed of "oak leaves, ivy, myrtle, or of flowers, violets or roses"[1]. It was a composite wreath, made up of all sorts of colours, textures and shapes. Such was the church, and its presence and witness were the seal and sign of Paul's success. That's how he saw them anyway. His joy and crown was them.

Thought

A church flourishes when it knows it is deeply loved by its leadership.

Prayer

Father, help me to truly love your children, whoever they are.

---

[1]   Kenneth Wuest, *Word Studies in the Greek New Testament, Vol 2, Philippians,* (Eerdmans, Michigan, 1970), p.105

DAY SEVENTY-ONE

Agreeing in the Lord (1)

Phil.4:2,3

I entreat Euodia and I entreat Syntyche to agree in the Lord.
Yes, I ask you also, true companion, help these women, who
have labored side by side with me in the gospel together with
Clement and the rest of my fellow workers, whose names are
in the book of life.

Picking up on the phrase "standing firm in the Lord", it is good to note that the ground on which we are able to stand firm is in the Lord. He is our strength; he is the glue that holds us together. Without him, church is just a crowd of individuals. In him, we are a family, a body and a holy nation. Families are designed to stay together. That is why division within the body goes right against the flow of the work of the Spirit in our lives. Those who easily walk out of church have not understood what the church is. We are carrying something far deeper than the natural in our spiritual DNA.

Paul has given a general exhortation and now he brings a specific application. There has been a disagreement between two women – Euodia and Syntyche. Their names are significant. Euodia means 'prosperous journey'. A more modern terminology would be "one who has arrived" – giving a sense of a settled maturity. Syntyche means 'pleasant acquaintance'. In today's language, we would say that she was 'a good mixer'. These were good women; mature, likeable and well established in the life of the church. They also had history with Paul. They "laboured side by side" with him in the gospel. Kenneth Wuest wrote:

The word 'laboured' is a translation of a Greek word used of
a group of athletes who played on a team together, co-
operating with each other in perfect harmony to attain a

certain end, the word having in it also the ideas of strenuous and agonizing effort.[1]

They had contended together, with Paul, for the gospel, but now they were in contention with each other. They were, in all probability, two of the first converts in the church because it was to a group of women praying down by the river that Paul began to share the good news. (Acts 16:13,15)

We have no idea of what caused the rift – it is not mentioned. The way the text was constructed demonstrated there was suddenly an issue, whereupon the two women did not see 'eye to eye', and this sparked off a disagreement, leading eventually to entrenched positions. This was followed by an emotional and possible physical parting of the ways. In my experience, sometimes the initial reason behind rifts seems so paltry and insignificant that the following emotions and hot, angry words often obscure it. It seems to me that the Adversary loves to fan into a full forest fire any differences between us. Sometimes disagreements can come suddenly, almost out of nowhere, and that is where I sometimes discern the enemy's work. He seeks to prevent something wonderful that is about to happen. It is almost as if he throws a spoke into a moving wheel. Alec Motyer says something quite startling here:

> *Where Christians cannot bear the sight of each other, they will not be able to look the world in the face either.[2]*

The third thing to notice is that Paul did not give a verdict on who is right in the matter. Both women thought that they were in the right and the other one had got the wrong end of the stick. Paul came alongside, however, and entreated them both individually. The Greek actually reads, "Euodia I entreat and Syntyche I entreat..." He used a strong word, meaning 'to beg'. He did not command them; he begged them, saying please. A gentle spirit goes a long way in healing.

Thought

Forest fires start with a small flame. Get to it quickly.

---

[1] Kenneth Wuest, *Word Studies in the Greek New Testament, Vol 2, Philippians,* (Eerdmans, Michigan, 1970), p.108

[2] Alec Motyer, *The Message of Philippians,* Inter-Varsity Press, Illinois, 1984), p.203

Prayer

Lord, help me to discern what is going on behind the scenes of each disagreement.

DAY SEVENTY-TWO

Agreeing in the Lord (2)

Phil.4:2

I entreat Euodia and I entreat Syntyche to agree in the Lord.

Paul was probably remembering his own huge flare-up with Barnabas as he sought to handle the disagreement between these two women. Reflecting on how he had reacted then helped him in being tender with these two women now. Our past mistakes should teach us how to handle things in the future. In fact, the 'University of Mistakes and Failures' is a most effective place to learn the ways of God and about how He works in and through us. It is also where we learn the most about ourselves. The restoration of people and relationships should always be done in "a spirit of gentleness". (Gal.6:1) Have a think about how we would want other people to approach us, if we ever found ourselves in difficulties with another brother or sister.

Paul entreated them "to agree". The phrase he used is also found in Phil.2:2, where he wrote, "Have the same mind," or, 'Think the same thing.' The NASB puts it this way: "Live in harmony..." The NIV Commentary renders it, "Bring your attitudes into harmony."

I find a number of things here.

Firstly, our personal differences can actually prove harmful to the testimony of the church and the kingdom. Paul was urging them to see a far bigger picture than that of their own personal issues. The good of the church needed to rise above and become pre-eminent in their thinking. They both needed to be asking, what is this doing to the testimony of the Church and to the name of Christ? This is always good ground for seeking reconciliation. In this context, holding grudges and resentment can become purely selfish behaviour.

Secondly, concerning the issues, we do not always need to have the same point of view. We must learn to value the other point of view. Michael Casey, a Benedictine monk, in his very powerful book *Truthful Living – St Benedict's teaching on humility,* says that we need to learn how to put a distance between ourselves and our natural defensiveness – in that way, we might just "come to the point of accepting that there is a certain reasonableness in [the other person's] negative assessment of

166

[us]"[1]. In other words, the other point of view just might have some truth in it. Real humility will want to learn what that truth or insight might be.

In order to achieve a harmony, there should be two or more different notes playing the same piece of music, and from the same page. Harmony is the mingling of notes. Paul was asking these two women to see the bigger picture and to work at harmonizing their different thoughts in order to achieve a greater insight. I do not believe that every time there is a tension in our relationships, that it is brought with deliberate and malicious intent. Most of these things are down to not seeing the same thing the same way. This is part of the way we grow, by learning to appreciate a different point of view. It is only hurt and defensiveness that prevents the process. We need to learn to give room to, and appreciate, the other person's perspective.

Thought

To insist that my point of view is the only valid one is at best arrogant and at worst damaging to meaningful relationships.

Prayer

Please, Lord, open my eyes to see what others are seeing.

---

[1]   Michael Casey OSB, *Truthful Living,* (Gracewing, Leominster, 2001), p.19

DAY SEVENTY-THREE

Help These Women

Phil.4:3

Yes, I ask you also, true companion, help these women, who have labored side by side with me in the gospel together with Clement and the rest of my fellow workers, whose names are in the book of life.

These two individuals had fallen out, and Paul was gently coming alongside each of them to ask them to put their seemingly opposing views into a harmony in the Lord. Paul "entreated" them (ESV), "urged" them (The Message), "appealed" (NLT). The word he actually used in addressing them was *parakaleō*, meaning 'to call to one's side'. This makes me think of the Holy Spirit, who is also called the *paraklētos* – 'the One called alongside'. Can I emphasise again that the ministry of the Spirit is to bring us all into a deep harmony of life together, and he is constantly waiting in the wings, as it were, to help in this process wherever there is disagreement. Paul, in the tenor of the Spirit, was coming alongside these women.

Paul then turned to 'another' to help these two women. It is uncertain who this person was, and maybe this was deliberate. Many have sought to identify the individual and the attempts have ranged from the probable to the ridiculous. The two words used, *gnēsie sunzuge*, meant 'genuine co-worker, colleague or team-player'. Paul was reaching out to an individual, any individual in fact, who truly understood people and team dynamics, and was saying to him, "Don't duck this and say that it doesn't concern you. Knowing the effect this can have in your church, if you see it, gently get involved and help these two to come to a harmony."

The word translated "help" here is actually quite strong – it is *sunlambanou*, and it properly meant 'to seize, to take hold of, to clasp'. The thought was that those around were not to sit there silently, hoping that it will all blow over and go away, but that they were to seriously engage with, and grasp hold of, these two individuals with a view to seeing them walking together and functioning together again.

The fact that Paul wrote "help" rather than "insist" suggests that these two women were already seeking to find a resolution but had got stuck a little. This genuine team-player was to enter into a process maybe already started and bring a far more objective point of view. The third view can often be the most fruitful in this kind of situation.

Paul went on to mention Clement and also "the rest of my fellow workers" – the other team members. We are not sure who Clement is, or who the nameless others are either. I'm not sure that it matters, because Paul says that their names are written in "the book of life". This book – the Book of Life – is mentioned several times in the Scriptures and is unique. It holds all the names of those who belong to the Lord, and it was written before creation. We were known in heaven before we were known in the earth. Although these people may have been unknown to us, they were known in heaven. Our service for the Lord may well pass un-noticed here, but not in heaven. There, it is noticed, and it shall be commented upon. One commentator wrote of these nameless team players:

> *Their names have a glory greater than that of historical renown.*[1]

This is a spiritually healthy perspective – we do not serve for the comments of men; in all our serving, it is for him, and for his comments.

Thought

Today, lift your head above your own circumstances, and look out for those who are struggling with relational issues. If you can, get alongside them with a "Can I help?"

Prayer

Lord, help me to reach out in the tenor of your Spirit to others today.

---

[1] Kennedy, cited by Jac Müller, *The Epistles of Paul to the Philippians and to Philemon,* (Eerdmans, Michigan, 1980), p.139

DAY SEVENTY-FOUR

Rejoice in the Lord

Phil.4:4

Rejoice in the Lord always; again I will say, rejoice.

What do you say to a group of believers who are living under persecution, and are suffering for their faith? What do you say to a church that is walking through pain and divisions? The word that Paul chose to drop in right here was "rejoice", and he repeated it for emphasis. It came suddenly into his letter with startling effect. Surely here he had got the wrong word! It should have been words such as, "Persevere and don't give up!" "Trust and have faith!" or even, "I understand and I'm with you in this." But no, he chose the word "rejoice". This was not callous, this was calculated.

My mind goes to something the apostle Peter wrote to another group of suffering believers: "Though you have not seen him, you love him. Though you do not now see him, you believe in him and rejoice with joy that is inexpressible and filled with glory..." (1.Pet.1:8) I love the KJV rendering: "Ye rejoice with joy unspeakable..." What was this?

For Paul to repeat the command – for that is what it was; it was not a suggestion – must have seemed unreasonable and unfair, and possibly quite unfeeling, given the conditions in the church. But Paul had seen something and wanted them to see it as well. He had seen that although circumstances can change swiftly for the worse, there was one seated in heaven, immoveable, unshakeable and who laughs at the attempts of the enemy to bring damage to his kingdom. Albert Barnes wrote:

> *If everything else changes, yet the Lord does not change; if the sources of all other joy are dried up, yet this is not; and there is not a moment of a Christian's life in which he may not find joy in the character, law, and promises of God.[1]*

The Preacher's commentary says:

---

[1] *Albert Barnes's Notes on the Bible,* e-sword.net

The joy of the Christian is not a passing quality. Rejoicing is not to be reserved for special times of worship or praise. It is to be uninterrupted and unbroken.[1]

Paul was saying that whatever the circumstances, they needed to rejoice. And so for us, in spite of everything that is happening within us and around us, we too need to rejoice. The strong lesson here is that our circumstances must never be allowed to determine the state of our soul – our hearts and our minds.

Because we belong to Christ, we are of a different order. There are things now set in place into our lives that are unshakeable. We are in Christ, and this is the sphere where this joy is found and experienced. It does not come naturally; but in Christ, we are not merely natural. We have his Spirit within us and live under the constant loving gaze and care of a Father who has our best interests at heart. Because we are rooted in him, founded upon a rock, the winds and storms that destroy others will not destroy us. P. Bonnard wrote:

The Pauline appeals to joy are never simply encouragements; they throw back the distressed church on their Lord; they are, above all, appeals to faith.[2]

Dire circumstances should be forcing us to ask ourselves, what exactly do I see and believe? What we see, what we believe and what we think should cause a song to arise from within.

Thought

Holy laughter in the face of the enemy is God-like. Look at Psa.2:4 / Psa.37:13 / Psa.59:8.

Prayer

Father, give me your perspective today on what is threatening me.

---

[1]   *The Preacher's Commentary,* e-sword.net
[2]   P. Bonnard, cited by Ralph Martin, *The Epistle of Paul to the Philippians,* (Tyndale Press, London, 1963), p.167

DAY SEVENTY-FIVE

Sweet Reasonableness

Phil.4:5

Let your reasonableness be known to everyone. The Lord is at hand...

The command that comes to us to rejoice should not drive us to bury our heads in the sand with despair; rather it should encourage us to lift our head, heart and soul to heaven. The Baker's New Testament commentary says:

> *It was not unreasonable for Paul to exhort the Philippians to rejoice, for the disposition of joy can be and should be cultivated.*[1]

In difficult times we have a responsibility and an opportunity to exhibit the extraordinary life of the kingdom.

Paul went on to write, "Let your reasonableness be known to everyone." The NASB has it "forbearing spirit". The NIV has "gentleness". Matthew Arnold translates it "your sweet reasonableness"[2]. The Message has this interesting rendition: "Make it as clear as you can to all you meet that you're on their side, working with them and not against them." The Geneva Bible has "the patient mind". One commentator[3] puts "big-heartedness". The word is *epieikes*, and it is very difficult to translate it into English. That is why I have given you a selection of good attempts to give an idea of what the word actually means.

The best constructs on the word suggest that it is the spirit of an individual that refuses to retaliate when under personal attack and demonstrates compassion towards the faults and failings of others. This is a crucial attitude when we are seeking to maintain unity and a sense of community. With such individuals, there is a softness and gentleness of heart and spirit about them. But this is no soft or insipid virtue, says the

---

[1]   *Baker's New Testament Commentary,* e-sword.net
[2]   Cited in *Robertson's Word Pictures,* e-sword.net
[3]   *Baker's New Testament Commentary,* e-sword.net

Preacher's commentary, "but rather a bent of character that controls our capacity for rage and activates our capacity to love"[1]. The root of the word *epieikes* means 'to yield, to give way'. Are some of us unyielding, thinking it a virtue? Often, it can be stubbornness.

G.K. Chesterton speaks of the difference between 'crustaceans' and 'vertebrates'. Crustaceans (crabs, lobsters) are not nice creatures. Their bones are on the outside – visible and hard. They are 'crusty'. Vertebrates, on the other hand, have their bones on the inside. On the outside they are soft, but their strength in on the inside. They are very flexible, but they have strength. They can be touched and held without people getting hurt. The gentle man is not a crusty individual. He is gentle to the touch, and his touch is gentle, but there is strength to be felt within him.

The fact that the apostle says that this quality is to be manifested to "all men" demonstrates clearly that it is not to be contained within the church. This should be a constant in our dealings with all whom we meet, within church walls, and within offices and shop floors. It is what sets us apart as the sons and daughters of the kingdom. We, of all people, should be the most reasonable and easy to get on with.

Paul then adds, "The Lord is at hand." He does this to remind us that at any time he could be here among us, watching, listening and observing. This is quite an incentive to keeping our relationships sweet. Let him put his finger to your mouth.

Thought

In all our relationships with others, what is the one thing we are known for?

Prayer

Lord, make me to be a gentle, magnanimous and approachable individual.

---

[1] *The Preacher's Commentary,* e-sword.net

DAY SEVENTY-SIX

Dealing with Anxiety (1)

Phil.4:6,7

...do not be anxious about anything, but in everything by prayer and supplication with thanksgiving let your requests be made known to God. And the peace of God, which surpasses all understanding, will guard your hearts and your minds in Christ Jesus.

Anxiety is strange: it afflicts all of us from time to time, and can be quite overwhelming. A helpful piece of Scripture is to be found in Psa.94:17-19: "If the LORD had not been my help, my soul would soon have lived in the land of silence. When I thought, 'My foot slips,' your steadfast love, O LORD, held me up. When the cares of my heart are many, your consolations cheer my soul." The NASB reads, "When my anxious thoughts multiply within me..." The phrase "the cares of my heart" is the Hebrew word *sar'aph*, which means 'anxious and disquieting thoughts'. Also, the words "cheer my soul" literally mean 'soothe my soul'. The presence and words of God will always have a strong soothing effect on the troubled waters of our mind and emotions.

Here are some interesting comments. Winston Churchill, the wartime Prime Minister once said:

When I look back on all these worries, I remember the story of the old man who said on his deathbed that he had had a lot of trouble in his life, most of which had never happened.[1]

C.S. Lewis also wrote:

One is given strength to bear what happens to one, but not the one hundred and one different things that might happen.[2]

---

[1] Winston Churchill, *Churchill by Himself: The Definitive Collection of Quotations,* Edited by Richard Langworth, (PublicAffairs, New York. 2008), p 531

[2] C.S Lewis, *The Collected Letters of C.S Lewis, Vol.3, Narnia, Cambridge, and Joy,* (HarperCollins, New York, 2007)

Paul writes that we are to be anxious for nothing. The Greek is quite strong here and can literally read, 'Stop perpetually and habitually worrying over every little thing.' There are, of course, some anxieties that are understandable and rightful. They can be parental, pastoral and even personal. Paul wrote about the apostolic "daily pressure on me of my anxiety for all the churches". (2.Cor.11:28) Paul is not encouraging irresponsibility here.

Having said that, anxiety is a very human weakness, common to all, and is often linked to the 'littleness' of our faith. If we are in a situation that is giving us anxiety, we must ask ourselves, "Am I trusting God, am I trusting his word, and do I really believe that He is sovereign over my life and circumstances?"

The parable of the sower teaches us that the anxieties and worries of this world have a choking effect on the progress of the work of God in our lives. (Matt.13:22) Anxieties do not bring growth to our soul, nor do they increase the length of our life. In Matt.6, Jesus said, "Which of you by being anxious can add a single hour to his span of life?" Anxieties do quite the opposite: they diminish us, and can, at times, shorten our lives. The Preacher's Commentary says:

> *Jesus presents evidence that worry is irreverent, for it fails to recognize the God who gave us life and is sustaining it. Worry is irrelevant; it does not change things, nor does it help us in coping with problems. And worry is irresponsible; it burns up psychic energy without using it to apply constructive action to the problem.[1]*

Thought

> *Worry does not empty today of its sorrows; it empties today of its strength. If we are afraid, it shows us that we are not fully convinced that He really loves us.[2]*

Prayer

Dear Lord, help me to remember that you are with me in all of my today and in all my tomorrows.

---

[1] *The Preacher's Commentary,* e-sword.net
[2] Corrie Ten Boom,
https://www.brainyquote.com/quotes/quotes/c/corrietenb135203.html

DAY SEVENTY-SEVEN

Dealing with Anxiety (2)

Phil.4:6,7

...do not be anxious about anything, but in everything by prayer and supplication with thanksgiving let your requests be made known to God. And the peace of God, which surpasses all understanding, will guard your hearts and your minds in Christ Jesus.

King David wrote, "For the king trusts in the Lord, and through the steadfast love of the Most High he shall not be moved." (Psa.21:7 ESV) John the Apostle also wrote, "There is no fear in love, but perfect love casts out fear." (1.Jn.4:18) J.B. Phillips translated the text we are looking at today, "Tell God every detail of your life in earnest and thankful prayer." Peter the apostle wrote to the exiles in the Dispersion that they were to be "casting all your anxieties upon him, because He cares for you". (1.Pet.5:7) The writer to the Hebrews wrote, "Let us then with confidence draw near to the throne of grace, that we may receive mercy and find grace to help in time of need." (Heb.4:16)

Paul told the believers to stop being anxious. Instead, they were to take to God every single thing. Not just the 'big picture' issues, but also the minute and detailed issues of their lives. There was nothing that they could not ask him about. God is concerned about every single aspect of our lives – not just our spirituality, but also our everyday needs like bread and clothes and sleep at night. Often a child will chatter about things that some adults would deem to be mundane and unimportant. Our heavenly Father, on the other hand, loves to hear it all. There is nothing about our lives that is mundane and uninteresting to him.

The first step to allaying our anxieties is to acknowledge them, and the second is to take them in prayer to the Lord. That is what we should do with all our anxieties, but if we are honest with ourselves, it is often the last thing we do. Prayer is often our last resort. Paul uses four words for prayer.

The first word that Paul used was simply "prayer" – a word that was always used of prayer to God, from one who is lesser to one who is greater. It carried with it a sense of worship, awe and respect. The issue here for us is, not what we come with, but how we come. It also carries a sense of 'pouring out'. Someone has said that 'some of us are like bottles, full of churning, firmly corked up'. Don't wait for the explosion – let the anxieties trickle before the throne of God each day.

The second word that Paul used was "supplications" – and this described an intense desire for grace, for help. It was used both of 'man to man' and 'man to God'. It was a calling out for help, as opposed to the silence that suffered in silence. It is often our pride, and a false humility, that prevents us at time from asking for help – men in particular!

Then there was the word "thanksgiving" – where they were to 'mingle' their prayers with thanksgiving. That is why it was not at the end of the list. Every need, every anxiety, became an opportunity for God to demonstrate his grace, his wisdom, his love and his power. The sense of need was intended to become an arena for the help of God.

Finally, there were the "requests". These were the definite and precise prayers. These were not groans, nor general "bless me" prayers – they were specific requests. Jesus would often and specifically ask people, "What exactly do you want me to do for you?" We need to know what to tell him.

Thought

Let your sense of need become the arena for God's help today.

Prayer

Father, help me to see that you and I can handle anything life throws at me today.

DAY SEVENTY-EIGHT

Dealing with Anxiety (3)

Phil.4:6,7

...do not be anxious about anything, but in everything by prayer and supplication with thanksgiving let your requests be made known to God. And the peace of God, which surpasses all understanding, will guard your hearts and your minds in Christ Jesus.

Anxiety is caused by many things and affects us in many ways. The phrases "do not be anxious" and "fear not" are mentioned 366 times in the Bible, one for every day, giving the clear impression that the Lord knows that we are easily prone to becoming fearful and anxious at times. After all, we do not always see what he sees. The word 'anxiety' was rooted in a word that meant 'to be drawn in different directions'. It described, therefore, a state of mind that was at the mercy of distracting and conflicting thoughts, and its effect was to rob the victim of any firm focus. We must not allow anxiety to intimidate us, to throw us off track and reduce and stifle our journey.

Moving on, we remind ourselves that we are told not to be anxious, but instead to bring our anxieties before God in prayer. The text there literally reads, 'Let them [the anxieties] be known in the presence of God.' Kenneth Wuest makes the comment that...

> *...[this] is a delicate and suggestive way of hinting that God's presence is always there, that it is the atmosphere surrounding the Christian.*[1]

Isn't this what Jesus meant when he said, "I am with you always"? If only we could believe that very presence of God is the atmosphere that we live and breathe in, and that our prayer is not simply bringing all our anxieties to him, but it is bringing him and all his resources into all our anxieties, circumstances and pains! Wuest also says:

---

[1] Kenneth Wuest, *Philippians, Word Studies in the Greek New Testament, Vol.2,* (Eerdmans, Michigan, 2004) p.110

Anxious care is out of place in a heavenly Father's presence.[1]

So, we have done our part. We have taken the 'faith stance' of not worrying, and we have begun to take every little thing into the presence of God, who surrounds us. The Psalmist teaches us that he is a "very present help" in times of need. (Psa.46:1) Now we come to God's part. Having heard our petitions, what does he promise to do? What happens next?

Paul informed the Philippians that God would grant them his peace. He may not take them out of the difficulties, but would give them his peace, even while they were still in those difficulties. The moment they started praying, they were not alone in their anxieties. They shared their life with him, and therefore he shared his life with them, and his life with them became the dominant factor.

We need to remind ourselves that God is peaceful. Paul was not just writing here of peace as an abstract, but he was writing about the peace of God – a tangible reality. This did not mean that the Lord was detached or indifferent to their situations, but it meant that he was not tensed up, agitated or anxious about them, or about what was happening to them. He was, and still is, in perfect peace in and around himself, and he is also in perfect control. The question for us today is: do we believe it? Jesus also said to his disciples that he would give them his peace, and it would not be of that inferior quality that the world offers to us. The world is far from peaceful; it has no peace at all to give to us. It will, however, seek to offer cheap substitutes, at best superficial, having limited effectiveness, and very transient. So, when it comes to choosing the peace of God or the peace of this world, I know what I would prefer.

Thought

Do not let anxiety back you into a corner, but take a stance of faith in the all-present God.

---

[1] Ibid, p.110

DAY SEVENTY-NINE

Dealing with Anxiety (4)

Phil.4:6,7

...do not be anxious about anything, but in everything by prayer and supplication with thanksgiving let your requests be made known to God. And the peace of God, which surpasses all understanding, will guard your hearts and your minds in Christ Jesus.

We are still looking at this irritating and debilitating issue of anxiety. The text before us is such a rich piece of Scripture. Let me give a quote from the prince of preachers, Charles Haddon Spurgeon. He made an astute and very helpful comment on Psa.142:3, which says, "When my spirit faints within me, You know my way." He wrote:

The bravest spirit is sometimes sorely put to it. A heavy fog settles upon the mind, and the man seems drowned and smothered by it; covered with a cloud, crushed by a load, confused by difficulties, conquered by impossibilities. David was a hero, and yet his spirit sank; he could smite a giant down, but he could not keep himself up. He did not know his own path, nor feel able to bear his own burden. Observe his comfort: he looked away from his own condition to the ever-observant, all-knowing God, and solaced himself that all was known to his Heavenly Friend. Truly it is well for us to know that God knows what we do not know. We lose our heads, but God never shuts His eyes; our judgments lose their balance, but the Eternal Mind is always clear.[1]

Fear and anxiety desires to paralyze our faith, but our faith needs to rise up to conquer our fears and anxieties! John the apostle wrote, "For everyone who has been born of God overcomes the world. And this is the victory that overcomes the world – our faith." (1.Jn.5:4)

---

[1] C.H. Spurgeon, *The Treasury of David*, vol.6, (Marshall Brothers, Ltd, London, 1869), p.324

God did not rescue Daniel from the lion's den, nor did he rescue Shadrach, Meshach and Abednego from the fiery furnace, but he was most certainly in there with them. So often we pray for release, and all the while, God wants to enter into our prisons with us. When we walk through valleys and rivers, he is not at the end, over the other side, cheering us on; he is in there, with us, in it. The light is not at the end of the tunnel; the Light of the world is in the tunnel.

This peace of God, which Paul wrote about, was beyond comprehension. It literally meant 'it surpasses all powers of comprehension'. We can break it up a little in a word study, and it can read like this: God's peace is *huperechō* – 'standing out, rising above, going over the top of, superior to' – our *nous* – 'any intellectual reasoning or consideration and any particular way of thinking'.

Why do we find it hard to receive that which we do not understand? Does our restfulness only come with what we can understand or control? This peace is communicated to our spirits, and our minds, emotions and will then have to get hold of it. It is beyond our ken; it is deeper than our thoughts and feeling; it is the power of God being communicated to us.

Horatio Spafford, after suffering unbelievable tragedies in 1873, penned these words:

> *When peace like a river attendeth my way,*
> *When sorrows like sea billows roll;*
> *Whatever my lot, Thou hast taught me to know*
> *It is well, it is well, with my soul.*[1]

It can become a testimony. In anxious times, we feel we should be panicking, or going under, or inwardly falling apart or cracking up. But somehow, we are not. Somehow, we are firmly held in a peaceful embrace that we cannot explain. And both we and those around us are frankly amazed and astonished.

Thought

Perplexity or peace; the choice is actually yours.

---

[1] Horatio G. Spafford, *When Peace Like a River,* Complete Mission Praise, (HarperCollins, London, 2009), no.757

Prayer

Jesus, grant me today to bask, and to be bathed, in your restorative peace.

DAY EIGHTY

Dealing with Anxiety (5)

Phil.4:6,7

...do not be anxious about anything, but in everything by prayer and supplication with thanksgiving let your requests be made known to God. And the peace of God, which surpasses all understanding, will guard your hearts and your minds in Christ Jesus.

Today, we are going to round this whole section off. The prophet Isaiah wrote, "You keep him in perfect peace whose mind is stayed on You, because he trusts in You." (Isa.26:3) The word translated "keep" was the Hebrew word *nâtsar*, which meant 'to guard, watch, watch over, to keep'. In the text under consideration, the Greek word for "keep" was *phrourēsei*, which meant 'to guard, to protect by a military guard, either to prevent hostile invasion, or to keep the inhabitants of a besieged city from flight'. These words were military words. God's peace, then, was to act like a sentinel, mounting guard and patrolling before the doors of their minds and hearts, keeping worry and anxiety out, and keeping them from doing an internal runner!

You see, the areas that usually come under attack are our minds and our hearts. Let us pause here for a moment. The basic spiritual principle is that 'anxiety attacks' start in the mind, and if they are not dealt with swiftly, they then start attacking the heart. These unchecked and unchallenged anxious thoughts then start to make us feel anxious. And if still not dealt with, we will end up making decisions that are based on anxiety and fear, rather than faith.

Consider this wisdom from the pen of Thomas à Kempis. He wrote:

Often we know not what we are able to do, but temptation reveals what we are. We must be especially vigilant at the onset of temptation, for the enemy is more easily overcome if he is refused entrance to the door of the mind, and resisted at the threshold at his first knock. Hence one has written, "Resist at the beginning; if you delay, evils gather strength, and remedy is sought too late." For first there comes into the mind an evil thought; followed by a strong imagination of it; then a sense of delight; then an evil impulse and assenting.[1]

We do need to listen to these old masters of the spiritual life. Martin Luther also wrote:

You can't stop the birds flying in the sky, but you can stop them building a nest in your hair.

The undisciplined mind will entertain the anxious thoughts, reason with them, and then the heart will begin to grow anxious and fearful. Soon after, choices are made that are directed and fuelled by those anxious fears.

We must let our minds come under the renewing power of the word of God. There is a wonderful promise in the Psalms her: "Great peace have those who love Your law; nothing can make them stumble." (Psa.119:165)

This passage in Philippians ends with the sphere of this peace. It is "in Christ Jesus". We must turn away from human substitutes, and we must turn to him. Only Jesus is the Prince of Peace, and it is only in him that we will walk through this world with our hearts and minds at rest. We must be at peace: having peace with God, having the peace of God, being at peace with ourselves, at peace with others and at peace with our circumstances. Only in this way can we be true peacemakers, bringing a sense of God's peace into the lives of others, instilling miraculous peace into our surroundings and settings.

Prayer

Lord, please deliver me from any intimidation, and release me into an intimacy with you.

---

[1] Thomas à Kempis, *The Imitation of Christ,* Book 1, chap.13, (Hendrickson Publishers, Massachusetts, 2004), p.13

DAY EIGHTY-ONE

Thinking Rightly (1)

Phil.4:8

Finally, brothers, whatever is true, whatever is honorable, whatever is just, whatever is pure, whatever is lovely, whatever is commendable, if there is any excellence, if there is anything worthy of praise, think about these things.

Anxiety states are mostly initiated by anxious thoughts that come suddenly, are often random, and most definitely uncalled for. Anxiety states are also often initiated by what I would call 'undisciplined dwelling' on negative and wrong thoughts. Paul, in this part of his letter, gave us an antidote to anxious thoughts. Often in his letters, he exhorted the saints to take control of their thoughts and to direct them into certain paths. He seemed to have little sympathy for the soul that was dominated by negative circumstances and negative thoughts. He wrote to the Corinthian believers, "Take every thought captive to obey Christ..." (2.Cor.10:4) Eugene Peterson in The Message puts it this way: "...fitting every loose thought and emotion and impulse into the structure of life shaped by Christ." He therefore puts the control and the direction of our thought life firmly into our hands.

We have the promise that when our anxieties are firmly and openly placed before God, then the peace of God sets a guard around our hearts and minds. The word "guard" is translated from the Greek word *phrourēsei*, which is a military word meaning 'to garrison'. And so, thus guarded, Paul went on to give us eight characteristics of a good thought life, eight markers of a healthy way of thinking. He wrote, "...think about these things." The Greek phrase he used was *tauta logizesthe*, which meant 'to take careful thought, to ponder, to weigh up, to concentrate on these things'. This speaks of determined effort. Kenneth Wuest, in his expanded translation, put it this way:

These things make the subject of careful reflection.[1]

---

[1] Kenneth Wuest, *Philippians, Word Studies in the Greek New Testament, Vol.2,* (Eerdmans, Michigan, 2004) p.111

When examining our thoughts, it is good to ask ourselves some questions. Are they true or are they false? Do they have a ring of authenticity about them, or is there a hollow ring about them? Do they enlighten us, or do they introduce shadows? Do they appeal to our inner life with God, fuelling pure spiritual desires, or do they appeal to our lower life of sensuality and carnal desire? Do they inspire faith, or are they the harbingers of fear? We need to be vigilant here, examining and asking ourselves, what are these thoughts producing in me? We shall know them by their fruits.

The Preacher's Commentary says:

> *The body of evidence grows almost daily, yet every person has to learn the lesson for himself: we are what we think. Sour dispositions create not only sick souls but also sick bodies. Feelings of worthlessness, bitter resentment and self-pity diminish us to fragments. A possessive nature, self-indulgence, self-protectiveness, and self-centredness shrivel the soul, create dysfunctions within us, distort perception, blur perspective, and prevent any healing we need.[1]*

F.B. Meyer wrote about "the control of your thought, the government of your mind"[2], as if to say that our thought life is the seat of spiritual and emotional authority. Someone has written:

> *Thinking has a reflex effect on the whole character – our character takes on the complexion and hue of our inward thinking.*

The Good News Bible translates Proverbs 4:23, "Be careful how you think; your life is shaped by your thoughts."

Thought

What and how I think today will shape the next 24 hours of my life.

Prayer

Father in heaven, whatever is going on right now, let me think your thoughts after you.

---

[1]   *The Preacher's Commentary,* e-sword.net
[2]   *https://www.studylight.org/commentaries/dcp/philippians-4.html*

DAY EIGHTY-TWO

Thinking Rightly (2)

Phil.4:8

Finally, brothers, whatever is true, whatever is honorable, whatever is just, whatever is pure, whatever is lovely, whatever is commendable, if there is any excellence, if there is anything worthy of praise, think about these things.

Today's culture is replete with the love of experiences and encounters, as if they were the most important aspects of life. We move from one to another, hopefully finding the next one better than the last. This outlook on life, unfortunately, can infiltrate both our prayer life and our church life. Paul's words challenge our preoccupation with experiences, insisting that we start thinking, pondering, meditating and reflecting. It is not usually experiences that shape us; it is what we think about the experiences that actually forms and shapes our lives. Experiences are vaporous and transitory; good thoughts, on the other hand, are creative and formative and can have long-reaching effects.

Paul taught a strategy for a healthy spiritual and emotional thought-life. These were not 'positive thinking' exercises; these were biblical 'trains of thought' – and there is a world of difference between the two.

Firstly, think about "whatever is true". In other words, do these thoughts line up with the truth that is contained within the person of Christ and within the Bible? He is true and his word is true. The reason why we often get confused about what is right and what is wrong is simply because we do not know the Scriptures. Many are at the mercy of their own uninformed reasoning. Dr Martyn Lloyd-Jones once wrote that the most powerful antidote to error is a thorough knowledge of the truth. If we want to know if our thinking is true, then we need to expose our thoughts to the truth of God's word. Jesus said to the Sadducees, "You are wrong, because you know neither the Scriptures not the power of God." (Matt.22:29)

Secondly, think about "whatever is honourable". The word Paul used was *semna*, and it hinted at that which inspired reverence and respect. Vincent's Word Studies says:

There lies in it the idea of a dignity or majesty which is yet inviting and attractive, and which inspires reverence.[1]

When we think of others, then, are our thoughts honourable and esteeming? The word also speaks of a weightiness and gravity of thought, which will show itself in a dislike for the superficial and flippant. We need to recapture thinking great thoughts – about God, about his works and about his people.

Thirdly, think about "whatever is just". The word *dikaios* carried both the meaning of 'just' and 'righteous'. These, then, are thoughts that are fair: the kind of thoughts that God himself would think. These thoughts don't look for dodgy means, nor do they mentally rip people to pieces. They have a strong tinge of mercy in them, and a desire to think rightly about things and about others.

Fourthly, think about "whatever is pure". Like all the others, these thought strategies need to be cultivated, because they do not come naturally. They do not grow by themselves. We are all born with a tendency to evil, and therefore we need to train our patterns of thinking. The Bible is clear on this: purity of thought and heart are absolute prerequisites for an unclouded vision of God, and revelation wins hands down over guesswork every time.

Thought

"Blessed are the pure in heart, for they shall see God." (Matt.5:8) Purity of heart prepares the way for the revelation of God. Purity and revelation are purposefully linked.

Prayer

Dear Lord, help me today to get a firmer grip on the subject matter of my thoughts.

---

[1] *Vincent's Word Studies,* e-sword.net

DAY EIGHTY-THREE

Thinking Rightly (3)

Phil.4:8

Finally, brothers, whatever is true, whatever is honorable, whatever is just, whatever is pure, whatever is lovely, whatever is commendable, if there is any excellence, if there is anything worthy of praise, think about these things.

Right thinking was so important to the apostle Paul that he insisted that followers of Christ practise it. Their minds were not meant to be parchments that anybody or anything could write on, unchallenged. He held people personally responsible for what they thought.

In today's world, if we are honest with ourselves, much of what we believe is lodged within by how we have perceived life through our own sociological and philosophical lenses, our upbringing and our personal biases. We need to arrest this process, and start to become people who have thought through, and continue to think about, what we actually believe. The response of the Berean Jews to Paul's teaching was admirable: "Now these Jews were more noble than those in Thessalonica; they received the word with all eagerness, examining the Scriptures daily to see if these things were so." (Acts 17:11) This was not at all 'the hermeneutic of suspicion' that is so rampant today; this was the careful and eager investigation into the veracity of what was being said. These people wanted their lives built on truth, and God's truth at that.

The fifth strategy that Paul talked about was that of thinking thoughts that were "lovely". This was an old Greek word – *prosphilē*, and it is only found here. It meant those things that were friendly, pleasing, endearing and winsome, instead of that which was off-putting and repulsive. These, then, were thoughts that would bring a smile to the face of God instead of a frown. We need to remember that God not only listens to the words we speak, but he also reads the thoughts we think as well. (Job.21:27 / Eccles.10:20 / Isa.66:18) Augustine reputedly once said, "Guard well your thoughts, for thoughts are heard in heaven." Remember, it is always down to us to choose the content of our thoughts. Now that's quite a sobering thought!

The sixth strategy concerns thoughts that are "commendable". The word Paul used here was another old word – *euphēma* – and again, it is only found in this letter. It literally meant 'fair and attractive sayings'. These, then, were sayings and maxims that others had thought of and written down, that were worth collecting, storing up and thinking often upon. They would be good enough to share with others that they might think upon them as well. They would invite the comment, "I like that thought, and I would like to think that as well." From God, it might well elicit the comment from him, "I like that too, and I like the way you are thinking."

Psa.19:13 reads, "Let the words of my mouth and the meditation of my heart be acceptable in your sight, O LORD, my rock and my redeemer." It's as if David were saying here, "May the contents of my thought life bring you pleasure, O God." Matthew Henry wrote about the words that "arise out of the meditation of the heart"[1]. It would do us good to consider both the depth and the quality of our conversations with those around us, which invariably reflect the contents of our mind. This, again, is a challenging and sobering thought, and we need to ask ourselves, what are we thinking about? Is there any depth to our thinking? Is there any beauty to our thought life? What thoughts would we be happy for God and for others to know about as we think our way through this day? Think on those things...

Thought

God is listening in on your thoughts today. I wonder what he thinks about them?

Prayer

Dear Holy Spirit, make me even more aware that the Father listens in on my thinking.

---

[1] *Matthew Henry's Commentary on the Whole Bible*, e-sword.net

DAY EIGHTY-FOUR

Thinking Rightly (4)

Phil.4:8

Finally, brothers, whatever is true, whatever is honorable, whatever is just, whatever is pure, whatever is lovely, whatever is commendable, if there is any excellence, if there is anything worthy of praise, think about these things.

John Owen, one of the greatest Puritan preachers wrote:

The greatest sorrow and burden you can lay on the Father, the greatest unkindness you can do to Him, is not to believe that He loves you.[1]

What and how we think is so important, and our thoughts have great consequences. Mindsets are so important. They can cripple us or they can build us. They can bind us to the pits of earth, or they can take us into the courts of heaven. Paul wrote to the Colossians, "Set your minds on things that are above, not on things that are on earth." (Col.3:2) The phrase "set your minds" is the one Greek word *phroneite*, which means 'to keep on directing the mind'. Bishop Lightfoot wrote that "we must not only seek heaven; we must think heaven"[2]. The content and the direction of our thoughts are our responsibility.

Paul also wrote to the Romans, "Those who live according to the Spirit set their minds on the things of the Spirit." (Rom.8:5) Jesus once rebuked Peter, calling him a hindrance, saying, "For you are not setting your mind on the things of God, but on the things of man." (Matt.16:23)

Looking at this next strategy of thought, Paul wrote, "If there is any excellence..." The word here is *aretē*, and has often been translated "virtue". Paul used it only this once in his writings. Peter used it three times. Someone has written[3]:

---

[1]   https://www.goodreads.com/quotes/324326

[2]   Cited by Kenneth Wuest, *Colossians, Word Studies in the Greek New Testament,* (Eerdmans, Michigan, 1953), p.217

[3]   *Jamieson, Fausset & Brown Commentary,* e-sword.net

It is a term rather earthly and human, as compared with the names of the spiritual graces which Christianity imparts; hence the rarity of its occurrence in the New Testament. Piety and true morality are inseparable. Piety is love with its face towards God; morality is love with its face towards man.

These are thoughts that are morally excellent, and also courageous, for the word also has deep connotations of courage about it. True virtue is not passive but can be passionately active.

The last strategy is that of thinking thoughts that are "worthy of praise". These are thoughts that want to make you stand up and applaud. I love it when preachers drop a thought into their sermon that makes the congregation want to applaud. I have also observed others drop a thought and people have inwardly groaned and winced, and in their hearts they have turned away. Clean, lovely, in-depth and winsome thoughts win the attention of angels. Unclean, trivial and mean-spirited thoughts win the approval of fallen angels.

The Message version is good here: "Summing it all up, friends, I'd say you'll do best by filling your minds and meditating on things true, noble, reputable, authentic, compelling, gracious – the best, not the worst; the beautiful, not the ugly; things to praise, not things to curse."

Anxieties and fears are banished by deliberate, purposeful and faith-fuelled thinking. That was Paul's message to these believers in Philippi, and it still rings true down through the ages. Paul has given us guidelines for our thought life, avenues to travel down in our thinking, which will have a certain gentle beauty about them. As we deliberately turn into these tracks, we will eventually begin to reflect in life and conversation what we are constantly thinking about. We will actually become what we think.

Thought

Thoughts are like seeds; look to see what they want to produce in you.

Prayer

Lord, help me to recognise the thoughts by their fruits, and act accordingly.

DAY EIGHTY-FIVE

The Power of Example

Phil.4:9

What you have learned and received and heard and seen in me
– practice these things, and the God of peace will be with you.

We must never forget that the responsibility for managing our thoughts lies firmly in our hands, and we must never underestimate the power of our thoughts. This is not merely 'positive thinking'; this is 'biblical thinking'. The Bible teaches that the deliberate bringing of our thinking under the word of God and the rule of Christ produces godly attitudes and lifestyles. Holy thought leads to holy living.

Paul gave the believers eight great areas of quality thought patterns, saying, "Think about these things." He then moved from the thinking of great thoughts to the practising of a great lifestyle – that was to be modelled on the life of Christ. As a bridge for their thinking, he put himself forward as a living example of how life should be lived as a follower and apprentice of Christ. These were bold words, but we should remember that he was speaking to a group of people who had never heard of Christ, whose first and only experience of him was through the life and ministry of the apostle. Paul had no New Testament to preach from. In fact, the Gospels started appearing after his death.

Paul used four verbs to describe the process of authentic discipleship. He wrote, "What you have learned and received and heard and seen in me – practice these things, and the God of peace will be with you." The first verb was "learned" – *èmáthete*, and it spoke of 'the increasing of knowledge'. It was akin to the word *mathētēs* – 'a disciple, an apprentice, a learner'. So the desire and the willingness to learn was the starting point. The second verb was "received" – *parelábete* – describing 'that which is taken on board'. It is the assimilating and the taking to heart that which is learnt. The word learnt in the head moves to the word residing in the heart. The third verb was "heard" – *èkoúsate*, which simply meant 'to hear'. But there are different levels of hearing. We can hear words, or we can hear the voice. The final verb was "seen" – *eidete*, which basically meant 'to see that which is visible to the senses'. Paul was visibly a disciple, an accurate manifestation of the life of Christ.

The apostle not only taught the truth, but he also modelled the life. Matthew Henry wrote, "Paul's doctrine and life were of a piece."[1] What they saw in him, was totally congruent with what they heard from him. The power of example is huge – both negatively and positively. This is a huge challenge to those of us who have the responsibility of leading others.

The responsibility of the disciples, on the other hand, was to put into practice the things that they had heard and saw in Paul. Truth learnt needed to turn into truth practised. Our faith is a practised faith – we practise our faith. The word "practice" was *prassete*, and it meant 'to exercise and to practise repeatedly and habitually'. We need to learn to live and practise the Christ-life habitually and consistently. In so doing, we are assured of the abiding presence of the God of peace with us. He will walk with the authentic ones.

Thought

An authentic life – word and practice in congruence – attracts the company of heaven.

Prayer

Dear Jesus, may my speaking and my living today ring true in your hearing.

---

[1] Matthew Henry, *Commentary on the Whole Bible,* (Marshall, Morgan and Scott, London, 1960), p.665

194

DAY EIGHTY-SIX

Forgotten?

Phil.4:10

I rejoiced in the Lord greatly that now at length you have revived your concern for me. You were indeed concerned for me, but you had no opportunity.

Paul began to bring his letter to a close, and finished with some very personal remarks about the whole area of receiving ministry gifts. The text is a little difficult, and there is quite a wide spectrum of thoughts about what he was actually saying. The first impression was that there was a gentle rebuke in his words, that he was letting them know that he had felt somewhat forgotten. Unfortunately, this can be the experience of those in a missionary setting, when financial, spiritual and emotional support begins to dry up from the sending church. Words and gifts from the home church have such a powerful and encouraging effect upon their missionaries. Those we send must never become out of our sight and out of our mind. We must never let the 'sent' ones become the 'forgotten' ones.

The fact is that the Philippian believers had always been particularly close to Paul, and they had supported him well during his itinerant ministry. In the beginning of his letter he referred to this, talking of their partnership in the gospel "from the first day until now". (1:5) Sometime after, however, the letters and the finance had seemingly dried up. But this had not been neglect or forgetfulness, and I think Paul was merely saying that they had just lacked the opportunity; they had simply been unable to reach him. The concern was there, but where was he? We must remember that travel and communication in those days took a lot longer, and most commentators feel that it had been almost impossible to find out where Paul actually was. At the time of writing, the last gift from the Philippian believers had been received about ten years previously. But now, Paul was in prison, and now another gift had come, through the hands of a man called Epaphroditus, who had travelled nearly eight hundred miles to find him (v.18), and Paul was overjoyed.

The phrase "revived" was an agricultural word – *ánethálete*. Paul used it only here, and it literally meant 'to shoot up again, to sprout again, to grow green again, to flourish again'. Baker's Commentary says:

> *But just as in spring-time the tree puts forth fresh shoots, thereby proving that it is alive, so also the Philippians' interest in Paul had at last found a way to express and demonstrate itself concretely.*[1]

The Commentary goes on to say:

> *As soon as the news of Paul's imprisonment had become known in Philippi the desire had sprung up "to do something" to help him.*

The word "opportunity" was the word *ēkaireisthe* – again, used only here in this form – and it meant 'not to have a chance or opportunity'. Paul was therefore saying, "I always knew you cared, but you didn't have the opportunity to share it."

Today, we live in a vastly different world where words and gifts can be shared and given within hours if not days. Communication is such a vital part of church life. We must never allow people to feel forgotten. Prov.25:25 reads, "Like cold water to a thirsty soul, so is good news from a far country." We need to maintain contact, write letters or send emails, even little gifts and cards now and then on special occasions. Nearer to home, maybe we need to take the initiative and arrange to have a coffee with someone we haven't talked to for a while. Let no one ever feel forgotten.

Thought

The sense of feeling forgotten is a deep ache in a soul. Could you help someone today?

Prayer

Father, help me not to get so wrapped up in what I am doing today that I don't notice the forgotten ones distant from me, and the lonely ones around me.

---

[1] *Baker's New Testament Commentary,* e-sword.net

DAY EIGHTY-SEVEN

Learning the Secret (1)

Phil.4:11,12

Not that I am speaking of being in need, for I have learned in whatever situation I am to be content. I know how to be brought low, and I know how to abound. In any and every circumstance, I have learned the secret of facing plenty and hunger, abundance and need.

That we go up mountains and down valleys as we walk with God through life is undeniable. Things can go well for us, and things can also go horribly wrong. How we go through them, however, depends largely on how we respond to them and also how large God is in our sight.

The believers in Philippi were always totally committed to Paul and his ministry. The text literally reads, "You kept on being concerned for me." He knew their hearts, and that they were constantly rooting for him. He wanted to show them, however, that he was not in any way dependent on their giving for any sense of inner or outer security. In fact, Paul had learnt a wonderful secret over the years he had walked with Christ and his church, and it is here that we see something of his personal discipline in life.

Firstly, he had a correct attitude toward circumstances. These circumstances are quite variable, and there are two kinds: the ones we create and the ones that are created for us. We walk in the consequences of the circumstances we create, and we respond with grace to the ones that are created for us. Here, Paul was referring to the latter, however they came and in whatever shape they came in. The word "content" that he used was *autarkēs*, which meant 'self-sufficient', or even more literally, 'to be independent of outward circumstances'. This was quite profound. Paul was saying here that the world around him did not affect who and what he was within himself, because he had learnt to be completely dependent upon Christ. And so it is for you and me, that whenever circumstances trouble us, it somehow reveals our innate dependency upon circumstances rather than Christ to bring an inner security to our hearts and minds.

Secondly, he had a cultivated attitude towards circumstances. This kind of 'contentment' was not a special gift of the Spirit; rather it was a learnt and cultivated attitude, that came through the experiencing of many and various trials and difficulties in his life. Neither did it come overnight, but was a gradual insight that came to him, as one of those willing to learn it. The word "learned" was the Greek word *émathon*, and it meant 'to increase one's knowledge; to hear and be informed; to learn by use and practice'. Again, it was the root word from which the word 'disciple' came. Paul was discipled by the Master himself into this way of living. He did not get this as he sat at the feet of Gamaliel; he got this as he sat at the feet of Christ.

The personal pronoun "I" was emphatic here, as if Paul was saying, "I personally have learnt it; now, have you? Or are you still dependent on what is happening to you, or what others are saying about you for your inner peace?" The Bible is quite clear about this: responding correctly to tough times produces good things in us. James wrote, "Consider it a sheer gift, friends, when tests and challenges come at you from all sides. You know that under pressure, your faith-life is forced into the open and shows its true colours." (Jas.1:2, The Message) A real and authentic faith will learn and mature from whatever difficulties come its way; it doesn't moan about them but treats them as gifts from God.

Thought

Don't let circumstances throw you. Use them – as building blocks.

Prayer

Dear Father, help me to see what you are teaching me, whatever happens today.

DAY EIGHTY-EIGHT

Learning the Secret (2)

Phil.4:12,13

*I know how to be brought low, and I know how to abound.
In any and every circumstance, I have learned the secret of
facing plenty and hunger, abundance and need. I can do all
things through him who strengthens me.*

There is an Arab proverb which says, 'Better is a handful of dry dates and contentment therewith than to own the gate of peacocks and be kicked in the eye by a broody camel!' Paul was making a statement to the Philippian believers about his inner serenity. He was not reliant for inner peace upon favourable circumstances, nor was he inwardly demolished whenever things went wrong. His faith was constructed upon the rock-like Christ, who had become the true source of his inner security.

Paul had learnt a secret – the secret of inner restfulness in whatever circumstances he found himself walking through. This was not some kind of strange mysticism, but a deep serenity of spirit and heart that almost beggared belief. I imagine that it drew a response from those around him, saying, "Just how do you do that? How do you manage to stay so restful?"

This kind of restfulness is quite supernatural. The Lord Jesus had personally discipled Paul into this, and it had come by revelation. When Paul wrote "I know" twice, he used the Greek word *oida*, which was an ophthalmic word meaning 'to see'. This was 'knowledge seen', not knowledge learnt from books, or even knowledge learnt by experience. This was when 'the spiritual penny dropped' and Paul saw it for himself.

Paul also used the phrase "I have learned". The Greek word he used here was *memuēmai*, which meant 'I have been initiated into'. In other words, he had been 'introduced and dropped into' plenty and also poverty; into abounding and struggling. Christ initiated Paul into the full gamut of life-experiences, in order to teach him that none of them need affect his inner peacefulness. He saw by the Spirit that the state of his inner life was to be maintained by the Christ life within him.

He went on to outline this by stating categorically, "I can do all things through him who strengthens me." This reads literally, 'All things I can do in the one empowering me.' This was not some 'stoic or heroic' response to life; this was actually evidence of a dependent life. Paul was able to face anything all the while Christ was (literally translated) 'infusing strength' into him. The inference is clear: we cannot do this Christian life by and of ourselves. We cannot maintain an inner and restful security unless Christ is undergirding us and empowering us. He alone is our refuge and strength.

This is one of the most misquoted verses in the Bible. The context is that of being enabled by the life of Christ to be restful in whatever life is throwing at you. It is not some kind of 'carte blanche' to attempt anything and everything in the Name of the Lord. This is the ability to face all things, through the empowering of Christ. The word 'strengthens' is a continuous verb; this meaning that the strengthening, or the 'infusing of strength', is an ongoing process.

There is more. Christ strengthens us, not only to face them, but to smile at them, treating them as mere peripherals that have little or no effect on our inner peace. Let us press into him more, looking to him to gather up our anxious thoughts, to stabilise our fluctuating heart and to bring us into the peace that this world cannot offer nor understand.

Thought

I cannot do anything, but I can do everything that he commands me to do.

Prayer

Lord, open my eyes, and show me the secret of inner peace in all circumstances.

DAY EIGHTY-NINE

Learning the Secret (3)

Phil.4:12,13

I know how to be brought low, and I know how to abound. In any and every circumstance, I have learned the secret of facing plenty and hunger, abundance and need. I can do all things through him who strengthens me.

When Paul writes about the "secret", there is almost a veiled and somewhat sardonic reference to the secret knowledge of those Greek mystery religions where people 'worked their way up through various stages' to spiritual bliss. Alec Motyer, in his commentary, has Paul saying, "I have made my way up through the degrees of progressive detachment from the things of the world, its comforts and its discomforts alike, and finally I have reached maturity on this point. I know the secret; circumstances can never touch me again."[1]

This is the true meaning behind the text "I can do all things through him who strengthens me". It does not mean that anything is possible to me. Paul was saying that the disciplines that he had learnt, and the infusion of strength from heaven, enabled him to stand unmoved, at peace and in full control, whatever life threw at him. Deep rootedness into the life, ways and words of God will produce this. Let me remind you again of Psa.119:165, which reads, "Great peace have they who love your law; nothing can make them stumble."

The name "Christ" is inferred, being a later insertion into the Greek text. It should literally read, 'All things I can do in the [one] who infuses strength into me.' Kenneth Wuest translates it like this: "I am strong for all things in the One who constantly infuses strength in me."[2]

Also, the verb "strengthens" was a passive verb, which meant that Paul did not attempt to strengthen himself. Paul had learnt to be content

---

[1]   Alec Motyer, *The Message of Philippians,* BST series, (IVP, Leicester, 1984), p.218
[2]   Kenneth Wuest, *The New Testament – An Expanded Translation,* (Eerdmans, Michigan, 2004), p.468

because he had learnt to trust, and he was empowered because he had learnt to lean upon the strength of Christ. Hard graft for the kingdom of God is the result of received grace, not the means to bringing the kingdom about. Paul's own testimony to this is found in two places. The first is 1.Cor.15:10: "But by the grace of God I am what I am, and his grace toward me was not in vain. On the contrary, I worked harder than any of them, though it was not I, but the grace of God that is with me." The second is Col.1:28,29: "Him we proclaim, warning everyone and teaching everyone with all wisdom, that we may present everyone mature in Christ. For this I toil, struggling with all his energy that he powerfully works within me."

Albert Barnes, a wonderful commentator of the early 1800s, concluded that firstly, we need not sink under any trial, for there is one who can strengthen us. Secondly, we need not yield to temptation because there is one who is able to make a way for our escape. Thirdly, we need not be harassed, and vexed, and tortured with improper thoughts and unholy desires, for there is one who can enable us to banish such thoughts from the mind and restore the right balance to the affections of the soul. Fourthly, we need not dread what is to come. Trials, temptations, poverty, want, persecution may await us; but we need not sink into despondency, because Christ is able to strengthen us, and he can bring us triumphantly through them all. Through learnt disciplines and a deep-seated trust in Christ, we can be inwardly immoveable though all circumstances.[1]

Thought

Deeply rooted people are like trees; although they may shake in the wind, they are never uprooted.

Prayer

Dear Lord, be my source of strength today in the face that all that comes my way.

---

[1] Albert Barnes, *Notes on the Bible,* e-sword.net

DAY NINETY

Kind Partnership (1)

Phil.4:14-16

Yet it was kind of you to share my trouble. And you Philippians yourselves know that in the beginning of the gospel, when I left Macedonia, no church entered into partnership with me in giving and receiving, except you only. Even in Thessalonica you sent me help for my needs once and again.

Paul returned to his warm thoughts about the believers in Philippi. Anxious that they did not get the impression that, because of his confidence in the Lord, he had no need of their support and gifts, he repeated the fact that he was grateful for their help. In Christian ministry, there is this fine balance between 'trusting in the Lord' and 'trusting in fellowship' for necessary provision. God makes provision for us usually through the giving of others and not by pound coins raining from the sky into our back garden. And yet we are to develop a trust in the Lord, who can speak and inspire others to give, rather than trust on human friendships and fellowship. If our trust is only in others, we will quickly be disappointed. If our trust is truly only in God, we will never be disappointed.

The believers at Philippi were those who stood with Paul through thick and thin. These were no fair-weather friends. They shared not only his joys and successes, but they shared his troubles as well. The word "trouble" is the Greek word *thlipsei*; it is the plural of *thlipsis*, a word that meant 'pressures' – the sort that produced a sense of being uncomfortably squeezed. For us, this is part of life. Being squeezed under pressure actually reveals what is really within us.

They "shared" his pressures. The old word *sunkoinéōnésantes* gave the sense of 'being involved, sharing, partaking with' his pressures. It is the meaning of the old church word 'communicated' – in the sense of 'having communion'. They did much more than just see and take note of his predicaments; they reached out and touched him. His pressures become theirs, and vice versa, and they were felt, shared and experienced.

This church in fact stood head and shoulders above all others in Paul's eyes, in that they were the only ones to enter into fellowship with him in the matter of giving and receiving. This was a church which gave as well as received. And not just a 'once off' gift – there had been years of giving, sustained giving, committed giving. They had sown into Paul's life even though he ministered elsewhere, in Thessalonica, for example. This was not a case of 'out of sight, out of mind'; Paul's name was on their hearts as well as in their thoughts.

There are some strong lessons to be learnt here. Our current mind-sets are not conducive to long-term thinking about people. We can tend to problem-solve and then move on. Remembering, and especially remembering individuals, is a faculty within us that can be in danger of neglect and atrophy. Right at the end of his letter to the believers in Colossae, he wrote, "Remember my chains." (Col.4:18) The unknown writer to the Hebrews wrote, "Remember those who are in prison, as though in prison with them, and those who are mistreated, since you also are in the body." (Heb.13:3) We rejoice at good news from afar but can easily forget when times are tough over there.

Neither must we think either that the church in Philippi was rich. They were among those churches in Macedonia who struggled under enormous pressure, rejoicing in their suffering and generous in their poverty. (2.Cor.8:1,2) Their compassionate and sacrificial ethos was astonishing and truly inspirational!

Thought

Are there individuals that have been on the back burner of your mind that you could rekindle concern for? Is there someone you could write to?

Prayer

Dear Holy Spirit, please put back on my heart those I seem to have neglected.

DAY NINETY-ONE

Kind Partnership (2)

Phil.4:14-16

*Yet it was kind of you to share my trouble. And you
Philippians yourselves know that in the beginning of the
gospel, when I left Macedonia, no church entered into
partnership with me in giving and receiving, except you only.
Even in Thessalonica you sent me help for my needs once and
again.*

This church in Philippi was of a rare quality. They did not have a
vast missionary budget to support various ministries; in fact, they
did not have one at all! They were one of those Macedonian
churches. Here again are Paul's words written to believers in Corinth:
"We want you to know, brothers, about the grace of God that has been
given among the churches of Macedonia, for in a severe test of affliction,
their abundance of joy and their extreme poverty have overflowed in a
wealth of generosity on their part." (2.Cor.8:1,2) The words "their
extreme poverty" is a translation of the Greek phrase *hē kata bathous
ptōcheia autōn*. There are two words I want us to think about. The first
is *bathous*, from which we get our word 'bathysphere'. It meant 'the deep,
dark depths'. The other word is *ptōcheia*, which meant 'abject poverty'.
Kenneth Wuest translates this as "poverty which went down to the
depths".

William Barclay is very helpful here. In his treatment of the first
beatitude, "Blessed are the poor in spirit, for theirs is the kingdom of
heaven" (Matt.5:3), he notes that there are two words in the Greek
language for 'poor'. The first is *penēs*, and it described a man who had
to work for his living. The Greeks called him *autodiakonos*, which
literally meant 'serving and caring for oneself'. These two words
described the man who had nothing superfluous but worked with his
own hands to meet his own needs. This kind of spirit can manifest in a
man who wants to manage by himself, refusing any kind of charitable
help. It really is a wrong sort of pride and it prevents the blessing of God.
This is a man who God cannot help because he doesn't want any.

According to Barclay, the second word was *ptōchos*, and this was the word that Paul used here; it meant 'absolute and abject poverty, utterly destitute'. In Greek eyes, this state of being was shameful, wretched and pitiable. Plato talked of such needing to be driven out of view, out of the land. In the New Testament, we see the word being used to describe the beggar Lazarus, (Lk.16:20) the widow with nothing but two coins, (Mk.12:42) and the vagrants being asked to the banquet. (Lk.14:21)

Why do I mention all this? Simply because this church had nothing to give, and yet they were Paul's strongest supporters. How did that happen? Very simply, it was "the grace of God", enabling them to do things that were not humanly possible. In the same way, God's grace lifts us above the restrictions of our humanity, taking us into a realm of the supernatural. I can only imagine Paul's response to their gift, knowing where it had come from. He probably might have said, "I don't know how you managed to do that – I know how tough life is for you."

Many years ago, an OM (Operation Mobilisation) colleague spent her summer vacations travelling behind the Iron Curtain, delivering Bibles in her little Volkswagen Beetle. One evening, she arrived at a certain place to stay the night, and in the morning, after breakfast, her hosts pressed a large amount of money into her hands, saying it was for her petrol costs. When asked where the money came from, she was told that several families had fasted for a week and had saved up their food money for this gift. This was a demonstration of amazing and astonishing grace!

Thought

If you dig with grace into your pocket, you will find that God is deeper than your pocket.

Prayer

Father, help me to see what you see, and not be limited by what I see.

DAY NINETY-TWO

Beautiful Unselfishness

Phil.4:17,18

Not that I seek the gift, but I seek the fruit that increases to your credit. I have received full payment, and more. I am well supplied, having received from Epaphroditus the gifts you sent, a fragrant offering, a sacrifice acceptable and pleasing to God.

Paul had suffered with his full share of accusers and detractors – those who questioned his motives and 'game plan'. In a number of his letters, he had defended his stance of preaching freely the gospel, working with his own hands in order not to become a financial burden to anyone. If he received a gift, there were always those in the wings that would step up with accusing voices.

Paul actually demonstrated a beautiful unselfishness here. He did not look for the gift; he looked instead at the givers and what was happening in their lives. He felt that their giving was actually an investment on their part, not only into his ministry, but also into their own spiritual account. His eyes were on their blessing, not his own. The language here was quite commercial, and there was to be found a strong business sense in the affairs of the kingdom. Investment into the kingdom of heaven will always bring a return.

The famous passage in Mal.3:10 indicated the same principle. God spoke to the children of Israel, through Malachi the prophet, saying, "Bring the full tithe into the storehouse, that there may be food in my house. And thereby put me to the test, says the LORD of hosts, if I will not open the windows of heaven for you and pour down for you a blessing until there is no more need." The phrase "put me to the test" carried with it an almost legal and scientific terminology. It was as if God said, "Put this whole principle of tithing/giving to a scientific test, and watch for the results."

Paul was delighted, because their giving was a demonstration that, as Albert Barnes puts it, "their lives were governed by Christian principle, and this would not fail to be rewarded"[1]. In other words, their lives had been touched, influenced and shaped by the principles and laws of heaven. On this the Scriptures are clear. Those who give shall be enriched themselves. Prov.11:25 reads, "One gives freely, yet grows all the richer; another withholds what he should give, and only suffers want. Whoever brings blessing will be enriched, and one who waters will himself be watered."

The language then changed to a more spiritual tone – that of an Old Testament burnt offering. Of all the offerings that were mentioned in the Scriptures, this was the one where everything was given, without any expectancy of return – except that God was honoured and blessed. When the burnt offering was brought to the altar, everything went up in smoke, and the result, we are often told, was a fragrant offering that was pleasing to God. Paul likened their giving to a burnt offering. It had, in his eyes, brought much pleasure to God. We have to see that God understands sacrifice – more than anyone else. And when we enter into a spirit of sacrifice in our giving, it warms and touches God's heart. He sees that we have caught his heart and his Spirit. That's why Paul was so excited – he saw what was coming their way from such a sacrificial giving. Of course it blessed and helped him in his ministry, but that was somewhat eclipsed by the blessing that he saw winging its way from heaven into their lives.

Thought

It takes a certain kind of spirituality to be able to give without looking for a return.

Prayer

Father, help me to take my eyes and heart off the return that I hope for in my giving, and help me to look simply for the smile of heaven.

---

[1] Albert Barnes, *Notes on the Bible,* e-sword.net

DAY NINETY-THREE

God's Riches

Phil.4:18,19

I have received full payment, and more. I am well supplied, having received from Epaphroditus the gifts you sent, a fragrant offering, a sacrifice acceptable and pleasing to God. And my God will supply every need of yours according to his riches in glory in Christ Jesus.

The kind of generosity that carries the blessing of God does not come out of plenty, but rather, comes out of poverty. In Lk.21:1-4, Jesus had observed people giving at the Temple. He saw the rich putting in their large gifts, and then he noticed a poor widow putting in two small copper coins. He then made this poignant observation: "Truly, I tell you, this poor widow has put in more than all of them. For they all contributed out of their abundance, but she out of her poverty put in all she had to live on." Giving is easy when you are well off – but giving becomes sacrificial when you have little or nothing to give.

Paul had received gifts that came from people with empty purses, and likened them to fragrant offerings, which always attracted God's attention and pleasure. There is a giving of the regular sort, and that is a blessing, but there is also a sacrificial giving that alerts heaven in a way that the former doesn't.

According to the weight of Scripture, generosity begets generosity. Paul wrote to the Christians in Corinth: "Whoever sows sparingly will also reap sparingly, and whoever sows bountifully will also reap bountifully." (2.Cor.9:6) He also went on to write about, not the amount that is given, but the attitude in which it is given. He wrote, "Each one must give as he has decided in his heart, not reluctantly or under compulsion, for God loves a cheerful giver." (2.Cor.9:7) To Paul, such giving released something from heaven. Paul also hinted at it when he wrote, "And God is able to make all grace abound to you, so that having all sufficiency in all things at all times, you may abound in every good work ... You will be enriched in every way to be generous in every way..." (2.Cor.9:8,11)

This leads us nicely to our next text, where Paul wrote quite categorically, "And my God will supply every need of yours according to his riches in glory in Christ Jesus." (Phil.4:19) Unfortunately, this verse is often quoted out of context, promising an everlasting flow of provision, whatever. The context, we remind ourselves, is that of sacrificial giving. God will never fuel our selfishness.

Paul himself could repay these Philippian believers, but trusted that God would. Adam Clark had Paul saying, "As you have given to me in my distress, God will never suffer you to want without raising up help to you, as he raised you up for help to me."[1] This provision from heaven is always according to God's riches, which are more than able to meet every need. Nothing is beyond his capacity. Alec Motyer wrote:

> *His supply will not be limited to the size of your need, but rather according to (that is, in a manner which befits) his riches.*[2]

God's riches in glory cannot be fathomed or calculated. Our needs will never strain the resources of heaven. The combined needs of the world will never put pressure on the bank of heaven. Here's a thought: where does God keep his money? Usually, it is found in your pockets and mine. The big question is, can he call on it?

Thought

If I don't notice my giving, there's a probable chance that God doesn't either.

Prayer

Lord, help me to introduce a tinge of sacrifice into my giving.

---

[1] *Adam Clark's Commentary on the Bible,* e-sword.net
[2] Alec Motyer, *The Message of Philippians,* BST series, (IVP, Leicester, 1984), p.221

DAY NINETY-FOUR

Doxology

Phil.4:20

To our God and Father be glory forever and ever. Amen.

Referring to verse 19, D.L. Moody once described this verse as 'a blank cheque'. For him, the firm was "our God", the promise was "shall supply"; the amount was "all your need", the capital was "His riches", the address of the bank was "in glory" and the signature belonged to "Christ Jesus".

Paul had been writing about God's infinite capacity to provide abundantly for his children. He then broke out into an expression of praise. That, in essence, is what is called a doxology. The word 'doxology' is made up of two Greek words. The first is *doxa*, which means 'glory' and the second word is *logia*, which means 'spoken words'. Literally, a 'doxology' is made up of words that exalt and speak of the glory of God.

This outburst of praise was quite spontaneous. It was an outburst of worship. Although written for believers to read, I believe the writing of it flowed from Paul's grateful and worshipping heart. It is gloriously possible that as we saturate ourselves in the truths of Scripture, on occasions we will erupt in worship because we have seen something of God's glory in his ways and wisdom.

Johann Bengel (1687-1752) was a pietist and a Lutheran clergyman. He was also a renowned Greek scholar. In his view, "the doxology flowed out of the joy of the whole epistle"[1]. Joy is what real and authentic theology will produce, and that in turn will burst out into doxology – either borrowed from the words of Scripture or created in a spontaneous act of worship.

Dr Cameron, writing in the New Dictionary of Theology about doxology, says that theology and worship belong together. He wrote:

---

[1] Ralph P. Martin, *The Epistle of Paul to the Philippians,* (Tyndale Press, London, 1963), p.184

Worship divorced from sound theology or doctrine degenerates into superficial emotionalism. Sound theology or doctrine divorced from worship lapses into barren intellectualism.[1]

The two combined provide a rich texture upon which the Holy Spirit will build. Cameron also wrote:

A doxological theology, written in the 'the language of worship' (A.W. Tozer), seeks to join the language of the heart with the words of the intellect.[2]

Scripture is replete with eruptions and expressions of praise. Doxologies litter the landscape of the Bible. It does our heart good to look for them. In them, we see that the writer is expressing that all the glory and honour needs to be given to God who is far higher, greater and more wonderful that anything we could ever imagine. Doxology is an honouring of his greatness and almightiness, and a truthful recognition of our own littleness and limitations. All our efforts and achievements, thinking and speaking must always draw attention to him and never to ourselves. He alone is worthy of honour and glory. It is to be shared with no one else.

Thought

Read the Scriptures until your mind is soaked and your heart is fit to burst.

Prayer

Dear Lord, overwhelm and saturate me with your greatness, then give me voice.

---

[1] C.M. Cameron, *Article on Doxology, New Dictionary of Theology,* (IVP, Illinois, 1988), p.210
[2] Ibid.

DAY NINETY-FIVE

Christian Greetings (1)

Phil.4:21,22

Greet every saint in Christ Jesus. The brothers who are with me greet you. All the saints greet you, especially those of Caesar's household.

Paul had not quite finished his letter. I can imagine him looking up and calling to mind a myriad of faces. He was probably the greatest apostle the world has ever known, yet he could recall individual faces. Such a 'big picture' man, yet such a personal 'hands on' pastor. He says, "Greet every saint…" In other words, go round to each one, leaving none out. In his view, there were no favourites, neither were there any to be avoided.

Obviously, Paul had his detractors, but they were also his family. They say 'blood is thicker than water' when it comes to relationships, and that is true. One's loyalty to family should take priority over all other relationships. But can I suggest a little play on words here? Those who have been washed clean in the Saviour's blood, those who by new birth have become our brothers and sisters in Christ, should elicit from us a strong loyalty, whether they have upset us or not.

The English word "greet" is the Greek word *aspazomai*, and it has a wonderful breadth to it. It meant firstly, 'to draw to oneself'. We can all think of those we would rather push away from ourselves, but that is not the way of the kingdom. Our personal love for Christ is measured by the attitude that we have to "the least of [our] brethren"[1].

Secondly, it meant to 'salute' – not so much in the military sense, but in the sense of paying respect. Again, there may be those for whom we have lost respect, and our conversation about them is mostly negative. But is that fair? Is that how heaven thinks? I cannot imagine the incredibly beautiful three – Father, Son and Holy Spirit – furtively whispering together discussing my shortcomings – of which there are many. We must learn to show and express respect, not only to the greatest, but also to the least among us.

---

[1]   Matt.25:40 (KJV)

Thirdly, it meant to 'embrace'. All these active verbs have been used to translate the one word "greet" – a warm, affectionate word. In the family of God, we are all called to be warm-hearted people, not giving off invisible and frosty vibes to those we would rather not sit next to. In embracing every saint, however, it does not mean we embrace everything that they stand for, believe and practise; it means we embrace them as an individual, as a person for whom Christ died. I love this quote from Eugene Peterson concerning pastoral work with individuals:

> *This face before me, its loveliness scored with stress, is in the image of God. This fidgety and slouching body that I am looking at is a temple of the Holy Spirit. This awkward, slightly asymmetrical assemblage of legs and arms, ears and mouth, is part of the body of Christ.*[1]

"Greet every saint." The day that God writes us off is the day that we can write others off. Let us then learn to look at all the saints with the eyes and heart of Christ.

Thought

Large, all-encompassing vision must be accompanied by large, all-encompassing hearts.

Prayer

Father, help me to notice, acknowledge and greet all those around me today.

---

[1] Eugene Peterson; *Working the Angles*

DAY NINETY-SIX

Christian Greetings (2)

Phil.4:21,22

Greet every saint in Christ Jesus. The brothers who are with me greet you. All the saints greet you, especially those of Caesar's household.

The word "saint" is an interesting one. A lot of people equate it with those who are really holy, who have done great miracles, and who have powerfully and movingly exhibited the life of Christ in their daily living. However, the word denotes one who has been washed clean by the blood of Christ and has entered into a process of what the Bible calls 'sanctification'. The saints are not the 'arrived ones'; they are the 'journeying ones'. Some have just started, some have entered heaven, some are lagging behind; none are further on than expected, at least by heaven's perspective. All of us are a work in progress, with many dealings of God with our inner life up ahead.

The word "saint" is translated from the Greek word *hagios*, which means, 'the separated one'. A saint is someone who has been separated out of this world and its values, into the kingdom of heaven and its values. We may live in this world, but we do not, and should not, share its values. We have been called out of the domain of darkness in order to live in the kingdom of light. God has hosed us down, if you like, but now he is embarked on a lifelong process of cleaning us up on the inside.

Another meaning is 'sacred one'. A saint is one who is sacred. In the first instance, he is sacred to God himself, and is held in high esteem – treasured and loved. That is why it is important how we treat each other. When we speak to and treat our brothers and sisters in a diminishing manner, we risk the displeasure of God, who has paid an unfathomable price for each one of them. Then, he needs to be sacred to himself, to treat himself as holy to the Lord. We need to closely monitor all that we allow ourselves to be involved in. If the Lord has cleansed us, then we need to keep ourselves clean – body, soul and spirit.

So, they were to greet every saint. Paul then went on to say that they were also to receive greetings from the other saints. This giving and receiving principle was, and still is, a strong kingdom principle. For it to work, both elements must be present. We are to give respect, love and appreciation to every saint, and we are also expected to be able to receive it. Over the years, I have observed that an inability to receive love or praise is an evidence of a damaged soul. Some saints are so scarred by life that when others compliment them or encourage them, they can go into inner conflict or panic. When the Father spoke those powerful affirming words to Jesus at his baptism in the Jordan River, it wasn't met with any negative reactions. A proper reaction is not unlike our reaction to the grace of God – we simply have to say thank you.

There was a whole army of saints who greeted these Philippian believers. There were Paul's colleagues, and then there was the whole community of faith, even some of Caesar's household. Imagine that: the whole Christian community were applauding, respecting, loving and wanting to embrace this little group of people who had so sacrificially embraced Paul and his ministry. Our little offerings of love do not go unnoticed in heaven, or in the wider context of the church of God.

Thought

We were cut out to be different, not to blend with the world.

Prayer

Dear Holy Spirit, help me to see that a holy uniqueness is a gift from God.

DAY NINETY-SEVEN

Christian Greetings (3)

Phil.4:21,22

Greet every saint in Christ Jesus. The brothers who are with me greet you. All the saints greet you, especially those of Caesar's household.

When Paul wrote about "every saint" and "all the saints", he was exhibiting a very generous spirit concerning the church. It has to be said though, that in his day the body of Christ was not splintered with the ridiculous number of denominations we have today. When he wrote this letter, there wasn't a Baptist, a Methodist, an Anglican or a Roman Catholic to be found anywhere. There was the church, albeit with the beginnings and seeds of factions already within it.

It is easy to discount the word 'ecumenical' because of the liberal theology that has accompanied much of it, and also because it has tended to work up from the lowest common denominator. However, babies must not be thrown out with the bathwater! Today there is a greater dialogue going on between the denominations that can only be welcome. The Baker's New Testament Commentary makes this interesting comment:

> *Paul believed very strongly in ecumenicity of the highest type, ecumenicity indeed, but without sacrifice of the truth.[1]*

We must actively look for reasons to work and pray together. It is our responsibility to pursue peace and unity.

On another note, Paul mentioned the saints who were found in Caesar's household. There wasn't much evidence of members of Caesar's family being Christians, but there was plenty of evidence to show that a number in his service had begun to follow Christ, and for some of them, it would result in the highest sacrifice of martyrdom. At the beginning of the letter, Paul mentioned those of the Praetorian Guard who had come to faith. Each day, a different soldier from Caesar's elite bodyguard had been assigned to watch over Paul. One can only imagine the results of

---

[1]   *Baker's New Testament Commentary,* e-sword.net

being a 'captive audience' to Paul for a whole day. Prison can actually yield some surprising results. Paul thought so, anyway. Just because people are restricted in some ways, does not prevent the work of God in them or through them. In many cases, it actually enhances the ministry, if only we would have eyes to see.

The gospel has sometimes been called the subversive gospel, and so it is. The kingdom is likened to yeast that quietly, yet effectively, infiltrates the whole. The reigning power in Paul's day was Rome, and on the throne was a dangerous and mentally volatile tyrant. Nero went down in history as one of the most deranged and evil men that stalked the earth. And yet, seeds were being sown – yeast was being introduced. A.T. Robertson, a renowned Greek scholar, puts it this way:

> *Christianity has begun to undermine the throne of the Caesars. Someday a Christian will sit on this throne. The gospel works upward from the lower classes. It was so at Corinth and in Rome. It is true today. It is doubtful if Nero had yet heard of Paul for his case may have been dismissed by lapse of time. But this obscure prisoner who has planted the gospel in Caesar's household has won more eternal fame and power than all the Caesars combined. Nero will commit suicide shortly after Paul has been executed. Nero's star went down and Paul's rose and rises still.*[1]

The seeds of the gospel are so powerful in their working in the hearts of men and women.

Thought

A dropped acorn can grow into a mighty oak tree.

Prayer

Father, keep me faithful in dropping seeds. Some will eventually take root.

---

[1] *Robertson's Word Pictures,* e-sword.net

DAY NINETY-EIGHT

Grace

Phil.4:23

The grace of the Lord Jesus Christ be with your spirit.

The word "grace" was most probably Paul's favourite word, and certainly featured large in his thinking and experience. He lived and breathed in grace. Grace was the fresh air of God that had cleansed him and then animated him. I imagine that during the three days of darkness after his strong encounter with Christ on the Damascus road, he began to realise what a misguided wretch he had been. The damage he had done to countless families, the church, and even the pain he had caused Christ, must have hit him like a sledgehammer. Years later he wrote to Timothy, "But I received mercy because I had acted ignorantly in unbelief, and the grace of our Lord overflowed for me with the faith and love that are in Christ Jesus." (1.Tim.1:13,14) He also wrote to the believers at Corinth, "For I am the least of the apostles, unworthy to be called an apostle, because I persecuted the church of God. But by the grace of God I am what I am, and his grace toward me was not in vain." (1.Cor.15:10)

As we trace Paul's spiritual journey, we will discover that the more he walked with Christ, the more he had become aware of his own lacks, and also of the magnitude of God's grace. In the world, the more we know, the stronger we become. In the kingdom of heaven, however, the more we know, the more dependent we become.

At this end of this remarkable letter, to an even more remarkable group of believers, Paul spoke "grace" to them. Note that it was the grace of the Lord Jesus Christ into their spirits. This was both an unusual and a wonderful use of words. The grace that Paul wrote of was the animating, uplifting and enabling ability of God that took the believer out of human frailty into divine strength. It lifted one up into new dimensions of life, absolutely unreachable to those who relied on their own strengths and abilities. And it was all directed to one's spirit – that inner God-given faculty that, once awakened, was and is able to both recognise and apprehend the things of God. Through our physical bodies, we experience the rushing world around us; through our spirits, we encounter and hear and perceive the voice, the movements and the activity of God. In other words, Paul wrote to this church, "May the grace of the Lord touch and animate your spirits. May this grace be with your spirits, accompanying you on your journey, taking you to places you never thought possible, enabling you to do things you thought impossible."

Reliance upon the grace of God is the only way to make progress in the spiritual life. Dependency upon the grace of God is the only authentic source of spiritual strength. This was a wonderful thing to say to a church that was suffering and was poor beyond belief. Paul was saying to them, "Only the grace that is found in the sphere of Christ can enable you to mount up over the things that would throw others down. Only the grace that is found within Christ can cause you to continue in the faith. By grace you were saved, and by grace you will journey, and when you get into heaven, you will look back and realise that every step forward that you ever took was by grace."

Thought

Let your "I can do this" be exchanged for "thank you for helping me".

Prayer

Jesus, your grace is simply amazing. I thank you today, and every day.

DAY NINETY-NINE

Postscript – The Letters of Paul (1)

Today, we are going to look at Paul's letter-writing as a whole. For him, this was no occasional pastime, sharing a few nice thoughts with his friends; rather it was a strong, deep and profound, and integral part of his ministry. We cannot separate the life of Paul from his letter-writing. They were so thoughtful and penetrating that they are still having a life-changing effect on countless thousands of lives. Paul is long gone, along with the churches he founded, but his letters live on. We are foolish if we ignore them. I want to equip us with a set of theological and hermeneutical spectacles with which we can read and understand them for ourselves.

Around half of them were penned within the confines of a prison cell. They can, in fact, be divided into two categories: 'missionary' and 'captivity'. Some were written 'on the road', as it were, and some were written 'chained to a Roman soldier'. Wherever Paul found himself, neither his spirit nor his ministry was tethered. In his last letter ever, he wrote to Timothy, "Remember Jesus Christ, risen from the dead, the offspring of David, as preached in my gospel, for which I am suffering, bound with chains as a criminal. But the word of God is not bound!" (2.Tim.2:8,9)

God's word, via Paul's letters, sprang from the prison cell and entered the minds and hearts of men and women, laying strong foundation for churches and maturing the saints. Some of them were written with joy; some of them in deep pain. All of them, however, carried a profound influence. These words of God, encapsulated in the writings of Paul, entered into not only their present reality, but also into the future, and they still are a powerful source for corporate and individual spirituality.

How do we read the letters of Paul? In what light do we understand the things he wrote? In order to comprehend what is written, we have to firstly get into the heart and mind of the man who wrote them. What made Paul tick? The answer is that Paul was first and foremost an apostolic missionary, and it is precisely in that light that we need to read his letters. This is the key to understanding all the theology and content of his letters.

He did not write as a systematic theologian and a scholar, although he was one, having trained under one of the best in the land. Many study his letters in that light and miss the heart of them all. He did not even write as a pastor, although he visited the churches he planted and knew many by name. Paul did not pastor these churches – he set up local leadership for that role. If we study his letters purely through pastoral lenses, we distort the heart of them all. Paul wrote out of an apostolic anxiety for all the churches. "…apart from other things, there is the daily pressure on me of my anxiety for all the churches." (2.Cor.11:28) Paul wrote out of apostolic concern.

Thomas Schreiner wrote that Paul "was a missionary who wrote letters to churches in order to sustain his converts in their newfound faith"[1].

Thought

Today, instead of an email or a text message, write a letter to someone and post it.

Prayer

Lord, help me to rediscover both the time and the joy of writing personal letters.

---

[1] Thomas R. Schreiner, *Paul, Apostle of God's Glory in Christ,* (IVP, Illinois, 2001), p.38

DAY ONE HUNDRED

Postscript – The Letters of Paul (2)

Paul was no 'fly by night' evangelist who saw many converted and then left them to get on with it. As Thomas Schreiner rightly says:

Paul did not conceive of his mission as successful if his converts initially believed his gospel and then lapsed.[1]

Paul was an apostolic missionary whose passion was not just for numerous souls and churches, but also for healthy, mature and enduring Christ-followers and church communities. Often, in today's successful missionary endeavours, where the new birth rate is seemingly higher than the natural birth rate, the criticism is usually that the work is 'one hundred miles wide and one inch deep'. The desperate need is not just for preaching the gospel, but for also grounding the new believers in their faith. Paul held both in tension.

His letters were an integral part of his missionary work. They strengthened, they rebuked, and they laid theological foundations that still hold true for today. Schreiner also wrote:

Paul's letters continue to be studied (and believed!) to this day because they reflect the thinking of a brilliant man who responded thoughtfully and passionately to issues arising in churches.[2]

Schreiner previously wrote:

What made Paul such an effective missionary is that he wrote his letters out of deeply held and thoroughly thought-through convictions.[3]

F.F. Bruce, writing about Paul's practice of dictating his letters, said of him:

---

[1] Thomas R. Schreiner, *Paul, Apostle of God's Glory in Christ,* (IVP, Illinois, 2001), p.39
[2] Ibid, p.40
[3] Ibid, p.39

As he dictates, he sees in his mind's eye those whom he is addressing and speaks as he would if he were face to face with them.[1]

There are two further important things to consider. The first is that these thirteen letters are the only ones we have from Paul. There may have been many others. Anthony Deane wrote:

Quantities of his communications were not preserved; either they perished by accident, or it did not occur to the churches which received them that they would be of permanent value.[2]

The second is that we do not have any of the letters that were written to Paul. Therefore, we are reading from one side of a two-way conversation. In his first letter to the Corinthians, it appears that he was answering questions that had been put to him. Here, then, we have to try to 'mirror-read', by seeking to reconstruct the situations from Paul's responses to them. Hence the importance of the reading and studying of both the historical background and the surrounding cultures in which the church in the first century found itself. Such reading is invaluable to a fuller understanding of Paul's letters.

Thought

If we skim the surface, we will pick up pebbles; if we mine deeper, we will find gems.

Prayer

Lord, give me the heart of a biblical explorer – probing the depths of the Scriptures.

---

[1]   F.F. Bruce, *Paul, Apostle of the Free Spirit,* (Paternoster Press, Exeter, 1977), p.16
[2]   Anthony C. Deane, *St Paul and his letters,* (Hodder & Stoughton, London, 1942), p.74

Bibliography

Books and Commentaries

Patrick Barry OSB, *The Rule of St Benedict,* (Paulist Press; 2nd ed. edition (1 Sept. 2004)

Nicholas Berdyaev, *The Fate of Man in the Modern World,* (University of Michigan Press, 1969)

David J. Bosch, *Transforming Mission,* (Orbis Books, New York, 2008)

Stuart Briscoe, *Bound for Joy,* (Regal Books, California, 1975)

F.F. Bruce, *Paul, Apostle of the Free Spirit,* (Paternoster Press, Exeter, 1977)

C.M. Cameron, *Article on Doxology,* New Dictionary of Theology, (IVP, Illinois, 1988)

Michael Casey OSB, *Truthful Living,* (Gracewing, Leominster, 2001)

Winston Churchill, *Churchill by Himself: The Definitive Collection of Quotations,* edited by Richard Langworth, (PublicAffairs, New York. 2008)

Anthony C. Deane, *St Paul and his letters,* (Hodder & Stoughton, London, 1942)

Annie Dillard, *Teaching a Stone to Talk,* (Harper & Row, New York,1982)

Charles Ellicott, *Commentary of the Whole Bible,* Vol.8, (Wipf & Stock, Oregon,1897)

Gordon Fee, *God's Empowering Presence,* (Baker Academic, Michigan, 1994)

Gordon Fee, *Paul's Letter to the Philippians,* (Eerdmans, Michigan, 1995)

William Hendriksen, *The Epistle to the Philippians,* (Banner of Truth, Edinburgh, 1963)

Matthew Henry, *Commentary on the Whole Bible,* (Marshall, Morgan and Scott, London, 1960)

Frank Houghton, *Amy Carmichael of Dohnavur,* (SPCL, London, 1953)

Thomas à Kempis, *The Imitation of Christ,* translated by George Maine (Collins, London,1971),

Thomas à Kempis, *The Imitation of Christ,* translated by Leo Sherley-Price (Penguin Books, London, 1952)

Thomas à Kempis, *The Imitation of Christ,* translated by Aloysius Croft and Harold Bolton, (Hendrickson, Massachusetts, 2004)

Homer A. Kent, Jr, *Introduction to Philippians, NIV Bible Commentary, Vol 2,* (Hodder & Stoughton, London, 1994)

C.S. Lewis, *The Last Battle,* The Complete Chronicles of Narnia, (HarperCollins, London, 1998)

C.S. Lewis, *Letters to Malcolm: Chiefly on Prayer* (Harvest, San Diego, 1964)

C.S Lewis, *The collected Letters of C.S Lewis, Vol.3, Narnia, Cambridge, and Joy,* (HarperCollins, New York, 2007)

J.B. Lightfoot, *St. Paul's Epistle to the Philippians,* (Hendrickson Publishers, Massachusetts, 1993)

Robert Lightner, *The Bible Knowledge Commentary,* edited by Walvoord and Zuck, (Victor Books, Illinois, 1983)

Ralph Martin, *The Epistle of Paul to the Philippians,* (Tyndale Press, London, 1963)

Sean M. McDonough, *Introduction to Philippians – ESV Study Bible,* (Crossway Bibles, Illinois, 2008)

Thomas Merton, *On Saint Bernard,* (Cistercian Publications, Michigan, 1980)

J. Hugh Michael, *The Epistle of Paul to the Philippians,* (Hodder & Stoughton, London, 1934)

G. Campbell Morgan, *The Acts of the Apostles,* (Pickering & Inglis, London, 1946)

Alec Motyer, *The Message of Philippians,* BST series, (IVP, Leicester, 1984)

H.C.G. Moule, *The Epistle of Paul to the Philippians,* (Cambridge Press, London,1907)

Jac Müller, *The Epistles of Paul to the Philippians and to Philemon,* (Eerdmans, Michigan, 1980), pp.13,31

Watchman Nee, *The Normal Christian Life,* (Victory Press, London, 1961)

Eugene Peterson, *The Message Bible,* (NavPress, Colorado, 2002)

Eugene Peterson, *Working the Angles,* (Eerdmans, Michigan, 1987)

Eugene Peterson, *Eat this Book – the art of spiritual reading,* (Hodder & Stoughton, London, 2006)

J.B. Phillips, *The New Testament in Modern English,* (Godfrey Bles, London, 1960)

Thomas R. Schreiner, *Paul, Apostle of God's Glory in Christ,* (IVP, Illinois, 2001)

A.H. Strong, *Systematic Theology, Vol 1,* (Judson Press, 2009)

Desmond Tillyer, *Union with God,* (Mowbray, London, 1984)

A.W. Tozer, *The Divine Conquest,* (Oliphants, London, 1965)

A.W. Tozer, *The Root of the Righteous,* (Christian Publications, Harrisburg, 1955)

W.E. Vine, *Vine's Expository Dictionary of Biblical Words,* (Nelson, New York, 1985)

Kenneth Wuest, *Word Studies in the Greek New Testament, Vol.2,* (Eerdmans, Michigan, 1973)

John F. Walvoord, *Philippians,* (Moody Press, Chicago, 1971)

Electronic sources

Baker's New Testament Commentary, e-sword.net

Albert Barnes, *Notes on the Bible,* e-sword.net

Patrick Barry OSB, *The Rule of St Benedict,* (Paulist Press; 2nd ed. edition, 1 Sept. 2004)

John Calvin, *Calvin's Commentary on the Bible,* Commentary on Philippians 3:3, www.studylight.org/commentaries/cal/philippians-3.html

Adam Clark, *Commentary on the Whole Bible,* e-sword.net

Easton's Bible Dictionary, e-sword.net

Frederick W. Faber, *Workman of God,* http://finestofthewheat.org/workman-of-god

Fausset's Bible Dictionary, e-sword.net

John Gill's Exposition of the Whole Bible, e-sword.net

Matthew Henry, *Commentary on the Whole Bible,* e-sword.net

The Preachers Commentary, e-sword.net

Robertson's Word Pictures, e-sword.net

Thayer's Greek Definitions, e-sword.net

Vincent's Word Studies, e-sword.net

W.E. Vine, *Complete expository Dictionary of the Old Testament,* e-sword.net

227

Other Books by Alan Hoare

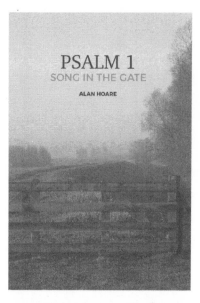

Psalm 1: Song in the Gate
ISBN: 978-1-78815-548-9

"Here is where we cut our teeth in praying, as we take upon our lips the prayers of others. As we make our way through the psalms – praying, singing, weeping – we will become more and more aware of the God who inspired them in the first place. They will bring us to both an intimacy with, and a deep, holy respect for, the Father, the Son and the Holy Spirit."

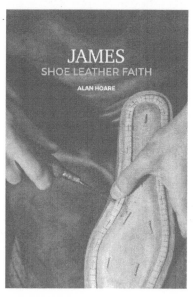

James: Shoe Leather Faith
ISBN: 978-1-78815-547-2

"The Scriptures must at times challenge what we believe and feel. The words of God not only heal and restore us, but they at times cut right into the core of our being, into the revealing of our hidden motives."

Alan Hoare's infectious enthusiasm for digging deeper into God's word is evident throughout this powerful 64-day devotional study of the letter of James.

Available now from all good bookshops.